It Won't Sound The Same Again
—
Great Jazz Never Does

By

JIM PHILIP

With

Trevor Bannister

2021

Published in 2021

Published by Springdale Publishing
34, Springdale
Earley
Reading
Berkshire
RG6 5PR
tabannister@hotmail.co.uk

© James A. Philip

The right of Jim Philip to be identified as the author of the text of this book has been asserted by him in accordance with the Copyright, Design and Patents Act 1988.

All rights reserved. No part of this book may be reproduced, stored in a retrieval system or transmitted in any form or by any means without prior permission in writing of the publisher, nor to be otherwise circulated in any form or binding or cover other than that in which it is published and without a similar condition including this condition being imposed on the subsequent purchaser.

A CHP record of this book is available from the British Museum

ISBN: 978-0-9564353-1-6

Design and production by Pageset Ltd, High Wycombe, Buckinghamshire.
Printed and bound by Print2Demand Ltd, Westoning, Bedfordshire.

To Nina
And for our daughters Jennifer and Tina
And for our grandchildren Luke and Phoebe

Contents

Introduction ix
Prologue xi

Chapters

I	A Scot's Enlightenment	1
II	Cutting My Teeth	11
III	And then came the tap on the shoulder	29
IV	A Change of Direction	41
V	'There comes a time in life which has to be taken at the FLOOD' – the Bard	55
VI	The Dunlop Star of Tomorrow	67
VII	Data Logic Phase 2 – Sale of the Century	79
VIII	Stargrove Enterprises	89
IX	Tales of The Funny Shaped Ball	97
X	The Youth of Today – Their Challenges	109
XI	And then the phone rang	123
XII	Dawkes Music – Back to School	131
XIII	Reflections	141
XIV	Epilogue – A Tale of Two Pianos – An Allegory of Life	147

Afterword 153
Appendix: Jim Philip on Record, CD, Radio & YouTube 155
List of Illustrations 167
Index 173

Introduction

On a July evening in 2019 the Remix Jazz Orchestra, directed by trumpeter Stuart Henderson, was booked to present a concert at Reading Minster of St Mary the Virgin – the centrepiece of the 11th Reading Fringe Festival.

Laden with his baritone saxophone case and all sorts of other musical paraphernalia, Jim Philip stepped from the bright sunshine of the churchyard into the darkness of the entrance hall.

'Was this the gentleman whose publicity photograph I had recently spotted on the Remix website?' I asked myself as I peered through the gloom. Doubts were quickly dispelled by the giveaway snatch of Scottish brogue as he greeted his fellow band members.

There was only time to exchange a few words; mine of welcome, Jim's in wonder at how I knew of his name. An explanation would have to wait until later. He needed to set up and I, as one of the 'Jazz in Reading' team promoting the concert, needed to find a home for a sponsor's banner.

The concert was a resounding success The record-breaking audience roared its approval throughout two-and-half hours of solid swinging music, brilliant musicianship and solos by turns elegant, moving and pyrotechnically charged, all firmly anchored by the glorious tones of Jim's baritone saxophone.

It was a far cry from the dingy, smoke filled room in the Students Union of Keele University, where, as a student, I first saw Jim Philip on a winter's evening fifty years earlier. He was a frontline player alongside Henry Lowther and Art Themen in the Michael Garrick Sextet which had made the exhausting journey up from London for the single gig. Jim didn't play baritone in those days. He impressed on flute and clarinet, and indelibly so, on his then signature tenor sax feature, 'Rustat's Grave Song'.

There were no solo opportunities for Jim at the Reading concert. As it drew towards a close, I began to wonder whether he could still summon the distinctive qualities of emotionally charged ferocity that captured my imagination so many years before. The answer came only a few months later on the Remix's home territory in Finchampstead, Berkshire during the first half of its Christmas Concert.

Amid the obligatory 'Yuletide' evergreens, Jim gathered every ounce of energy and emotion from the depths of his soul and took flight on an explosive sleigh ride – Charles Mingus' theme tune 'Moanin'. His free-wheeling solo led the band into raucous ensemble passages and group improvisations. This was it! Evidence of how the spontaneity of a jazz solo can transform a band performance and ignite the spirit of musicians and audience alike. The evening went from strength to strength and the packed audience left for home full of 'true' Christmas spirit.

You will find that the unquenchable light of Jim Philip's jazz spirit – forged in the Granite City of Aberdeen, sharpened to a cutting edge on the 1960s' London jazz scene, and destined to emerge undiminished from a lengthy jazz sabbatical in the world of IT, shines through the pages of this memoir. But remember, 'It won't sound the same again; great jazz never does!'

Trevor Bannister:
January 2021

Prologue

Family Heritage –
The Great War and Onwards

'Young Jim with mother and father

James Alexander Philip was born in Aberdeen Scotland on 30th January 1941. I was an only child. I started out as 'Jimmy' but over time have become 'Jim'. It appears that American composer and pianist Jim Webb has gone the other way and become a 'Jimmy'. I once wrote under the pen name 'Phil the Fluter'.

My father was Herbert (Bert) James Philip, one of **Four Brothers***.

The First World War took its toll. The eldest brother Alec died shortly after the war. He had been in charge of horses at the front and the wet and all the mud caught up with him. Bert himself saw his life 'saved' by his interest and aptitude in

---

*The Woody Herman Orchestra – Four Brothers (Jazz Standard)
Woody Herman recorded Four Brothers on 27th December 1947. Based on the chord sequence of 'Jeepers Creepers' it was written by sax man Jimmy Giuffre. The original 'four brothers' sax section in playing order was Zoot Sims, Serge Chaloff, Herbie Steward and Stan Getz as a homage to the style of Lester Young.

The 'Four Brothers': Bert, Sydney, Alec and Rich with my grandfather

early communications. Like most of the Scots, he had volunteered and was in Norwich training for the front when he demonstrated skill and understanding of early signalling. He was selected to follow this path, became an instructor and, as a result, avoided the open slaughter.

The younger Richard (Rich) was the only one to have a 'proper' education. He even went to university. The war saw him as an Observer in the Royal Flying Corps. Twice shot down, he somehow survived. Aircraft in those days were nose heavy and, being in the second seat behind his less fortunate pilot, he escaped with his life. He survived the war to become 'something' in the City of London and later joined the fledgling British Broadcasting Corporation (BBC). In his City days he persuaded my dad to send his money down to him for investment. Needless to say, all the money was lost in the 'Great Crash' of 1929. My father never forgot that and, to his dying day, was sceptical of the morals of the 'City Slickers'. Rich's marriage broke down and, back in Aberdeen, he went to pieces with an all too frequent 'bottle'.

Rich, fully clad in flying gear

The 'baby' Sydney was born after the war. He led an organised business life and was himself the proud father of **four sons.**

After the 'Crash' my father put his head down and grew a business at 32, King Street, Aberdeen. Called, the Camden Trading Stores, it offered a complete array of household products and drapery. He operated his business through a series of agents who attracted customers to the shop and its easy payment scheme. My father's worst job was to take his car round the estates on Friday nights to collect money owed by the poorer payers. He always felt in danger of a seaman returning home to find him receiving money owed from a fearful housewife. He once confided in me saying that on occasions he should have been *giving* rather than *receiving*, but that would have seen an end to the business.

Robert Gordon's College, Aberdeen

This led him to redirect me away from this form of life. He paid for me to go to Robert Gordon's College in Aberdeen and had an ambition for me to enter a profession and become a teacher. How times have changed! I fear that the once revered Teaching Profession has become a Union?

* * *

Chapter I

A Scot's Enlightenment

My moment of 'enlightenment' happened quite suddenly at a school Christmas class party way back in 1956. I was 15 years old. Stuart Miller, son of Bruce Miller, proprietor of Aberdeen's premier music and record shop, then located in one of the city's main thoroughfares, George Street and later, Union Street, was also at the party. He had with him the first 3-speed record player that anyone had seen and a handful of beautifully packaged 33 $^{1/3}$ long playing discs. We all clustered around while this wondrous device was demonstrated. What a great sound we thought!

We had been encouraged to bring along our own 78s so that they could be tried out. Willie Gauld thrust forward a Brunswick black label 78. From the speaker burst the high-octane energy of Louis Armstrong's All Stars and 'Basin Street Blues': Side 1 – the theme played with a subtle interplay from the front line … then Side 2. Well, from the high tempo drum intro the band just let go! 'What is that I enquired?' 'That', said Willie, 'is **Jazz!'** I was hooked.

The rest of the class moved into the next room for the obligatory film show leaving me to the music. The following morning, I announced to my dad, 'I want a clarinet'. This was well received and by 30th January, my birthday, I was the proud owner of a Boosey & Hawkes 'liquorice' stick. Cinema showings of 'The Benny Goodman Story' and a re-run of 'The Glenn Miller Story' only served to fuel the fire.

I obtained a sheet music copy of 'Memories of You', the Benny Goodman film theme tune and set about mastering the demands of the 'break' – the first major clarinet hurdle. By Easter I felt proficient enough to visit neighbourhood brothers Norman and Neil Simpson who played piano and drums. Placing the music on the piano we struck out into the unknown and the inevitable clash of keys. That night I discovered transposition and painstakingly rewrote the notes and staggered through a faltering performance. The Jimmy Philip Trio was born!

***

Up to that point my schooling had followed a traditional path. At Robert Gordon's College in Aberdeen I had enjoyed achievement in athletics. I was the Lower School Champion of the Coronation year 1953, winning all the sprints up to 440 yards and high and long jumps. I carried this on to the trouncing of the Aberdeen Grammar School's team in all these events in our fiercely contested annual athletics competition, a feat that had not been seen in living memory. The papers were full of it. The *Aberdeen Evening Express* even published a picture of my 4ft. 3in. high jump along with all the competition results:

PHILIP STARS FOR GORDON'S

An outstanding performance by Robert Gordon's schoolboy James Philip was a feature of the athletic meeting between the lower school, junior and colt teams of Aberdeen Grammar School and Robert Gordon's College at Rubishaw last night.

Competing in the lower school section, he gained first place in all the individual events except throwing the cricket ball.

Robert Gordon's won in the junior and colts contest by 75 points to 55, while the Lower Schools were level with 30 points each.

The Lower School results are shown below:

80 Yards – **1.** J. Philip (RGC), **2.** F. Smith (AGS), **3.** R. Watt (AGS)

440 Yards – **1.** J. Philip (RGC), **2.** F. Smith (AGS), **3.** M. Taggart (RGC)

Relay – **1.** Grammar School, **2.** Gordon's College

High Jump – **1.** J. Philip (RGC), **2.** G. Dunbar (AGS), **3.** R. Smith (AGS) – **4ft. 3in.**

Broad Jump – **1.** J. Philip (RGC), **2.** N. Ferguson (AGS), **3.** R. Watt (AGS) – **13ft. 7in.**

Cricket Ball – **1.** M. Dunn (RGC), **2.** N. Ducat (AGS), **3.** N. Dyer (RGC) – **161ft. 5½ in.**

Upon moving up to the seniors, I was immediately bettered by an import from Sweden – John Sjoberg (later to play professional football for Leicester City). I was severely chastened by this experience and my interest in training quickly waned.

Robert Gordon's, being a private school, majored in rugby. I possessed the natural ball skills to captain the Minors at stand-off but, as my physique failed to keep up with most around me, I found myself slipping down the ranks. By the fifth form I was resigned to being captain of the school seconds – **nae a place to be**!

Centre stage as Captain of RGS the 2nd XV

Mind you, only the best beat me. My position in the first XV was occupied by Ian (Spivvy) McRae. Ian went on to play for Scotland and indeed was selected as a reserve for a British Lions tour. Once, when asked by a fellow London Scot what I had achieved, I found myself saying that I was a 'reserve to the reserve' for a British Lions tour!

Upon entering the 6th form I approached my games master Ian Hastie to announce that Saturday games clashed with my new found aspirations in music. I shall never forget his dumbfounded expression at the news that I was off in another direction. 'Jim had obviously lost the plot. There was no hope!'

My clarinet teacher was the wonderfully named Bill Spittle. Bill, a Kneller Hall trained band master, had just arrived in Aberdeen and been appointed by the Education Authority as its first woodwind and brass peripatetic teacher. Bill recognised my wish for fast track progress and my ambition to eventually own a tenor saxophone. With great energy he formed the Aberdeen Schools Military Band (what would now be known as a concert wind band) and soon followed up with a big band. I joined the wind band and progressed to become leader of the clarinet grouping. Not having a sax at this time, my participation in the big band was limited to helping out by putting up the music stands and handing out and collecting in the music.

Bill had run a Station band in World War II. He described to me warming up the audience before the legendary Glenn Miller American AEF Band made its broadcasts from the UK. His description of gleaming Conn saxes and the skill of the US bandsmen had me drooling. I then acquired a rather leaky Buescher tenor

My dad's shop fitter and joiner, Jim Moir, ran a dance band – three saxes, trumpet, trombone and rhythm. This played the Friday and Saturday University hops – no Beat Groups in those days. The bars in Scotland at that time closed at 9.30pm so, although dances nominally started at 8pm, no one appeared from the Student Bar much before 10pm. Dad, being a typical dad, proudly announced that his son James played a tenor sax and before you could say 'Ted Heath' I was invited to sit in with the band.

Each week the latest dance arrangements arrived from the Bron Agency, London. I was given a 2nd tenor pad to sort out and joined in the evaluation of the arrangements from 8pm to 9pm. In those days, apart from waltzes and the mandatory Scottish dances, each arrangement had to be performed either as a quickstep or a foxtrot. The concept of people dancing to the natural tempo of the music fell on deaf ears. I always left at the break and went to the Aberdeen Schools Dance Club run by the indefatigable Madame Murray. Here, I immediately disappeared into the band room, unpacked my clarinet and joined in the obligatory rabble rouser – the 'Woodchopper's Ball'.

In action on 1st tenor (2nd from right) in the Jim Moir Band c.1960–62

My tenor playing and reading improved and before long Jim Moir invited me to stay on and play for the dance itself. This entitled me to wear 'the Maroon Jacket'. Mine had previously been fitted to a 'Gorilla' so my mother got to work with her needle and thread to turn the styling into something more akin to a double-breasted number. But oh boy, was I proud to wear it!

***

I was by this time finishing my schooling and had achieved an above-average university entrance qualification. In those days we were all expected to end up as aircraft designers or work for Shell Mex/BP, a joint company at that time. I observed however, that, as I was not in the 'top ten' in my 6th form, I might just be struggling to get my BSc 2:1. I therefore opted for accountancy and spent the next five years indentured to an office to obtain my professional qualification. What a grind – 5½ days for £2.00 a week!

All this meant that I was exempt from call-up for National Service, which had thankfully ended by the time my studies were over. I viewed this as a mixed blessing, for I once had a crazy notion that I could sign up for a term in the military and get into a band. This delusion quickly passed.

My teacher, Bill Spittle, continued to be a source of encouragement. He played lead alto sax in the pit band (*nae* orchestra) at Aberdeen's Her Majesty's Theatre and got me in on tenor and clarinet (also a little flute – that does not mean piccolo). I played for the Christmas and Summer shows – a complete change of programme each week! It was great fun and sharpened my reactions. Although Andy Stewart, Kenneth McKellar and Moira Anderson may not sound much, the programme always contained some challenging arrangements for the dance routines. I shall never forget the sheer guts of the chorus line as it mustered the energy for one last high kick at a New Year's Day matinee, with the boilermakers' children throwing ice cream cartons down from the 'Gods'.

***

Traditional Jazz ('Trad') was then on the up and up. I wore out my copies of Chris Barber's 'High Society' and 'Whistlin' Rufus' with Monty Sunshine on clarinet. There was no formal jazz training in those days. It was a question of turning up the record player and blasting along with it. Pity the poor neighbours, but at least we had a granite house in Aberdeen which constrained some of my excesses. Other clarinet players who drew my attention included the idiosyncratic Archie Semple with the Alex Welsh Band and of course the wonderful Sandy Brown – catch his 'African Queen'. Earning £2.00 a week supplemented by 30 shillings for the occasional gig, I spent it all on records. My collection of Benny Goodman Trio and Quartet titles grew, but then my friends introduced me to the world of big band jazz.

Ellington, Basie and Kenton all had their place, but I was drawn to Maynard Ferguson's 'Message from Newport' and 'Newport Suite' albums. Arrangers Slide Hampton and Don Sebesky seemed to catch the right blend of rich orchestration and exciting settings for the soloists. It was fashionable for the critics of the day to pan Maynard's screaming horn, but to do so overlooked the rest.

The film 'Jazz on a Summers Day' brought the West Coast movement to my notice and the music of Gerry Mulligan, Shorty Rogers and Art Pepper, soon swelled my collection. The band and work of Quincy Jones led me to the Thad Jones-Mel Lewis Orchestra, but it was the expansive palette of Gil Evans who, for me, opened out the orchestral context for the soloist to fully express himself. Albums like 'Miles Ahead', 'Porgy and Bess' and later 'The Individualism of Gil Evans' illustrate my point. In turn Gil led me to the genius of Miles Davis.

Miles was not an instant thing for me; I had to work hard at it. In common with many of his fan base, he left me cold with his electric thing, but from his formative days, culminating in the seminal 'Kind of Blue' and followed by his quintets with the Herbie Hancock, Ron Carter and Tony Williams' rhythm section, what is there left to say?

***

A highlight of the year for the Jim Moir Band was to dep for the resident band at the Aberdeen Palais Ballroom whilst the band took its week's holiday. Yes – a whole week, six evenings of continuous playing! After one such interlude, I was offered a position in the resident band; a chance to turn full-time and get my act together. However, my father prevailed upon me to turn this down as it did not appear to offer a stable lifestyle. A deal was struck between father and son. Once I had qualified, I could do what I liked.

The Scottish Chartered Accountant course was quite enlightened for its day. The Institute had introduced the Academic Year, whereby in the 3rd year all articled clerks studied aspects of law, economics and accounting theory full-time at Aberdeen University. What an opportunity! Still playing at the hops with Jim Moir, I also joined a six-piece led by an active student, Ian Stephen, with a trumpet trombone and sax/clarinet front line. We played everything from trad tunes to sketchy arrangements of originals by people such as Dizzy Gillespie, Cannonball Adderley and Gerry Mulligan, not to mention the underrated Benny Golson. I found myself contributing to the University RAG WEEK magazine as we had Kenny Ball and his Jazzmen appearing in the

Marshall Hall. Needless to say, he was well backed by the Ian Stephen Sextet on the night. Great fun!

At that time Aberdeen was well into jazz. Gordon Hardie had opened up a Wednesday night club at the Abergeldie Hall and we flocked to see what was going on. Sandy West's trad band led the way but there was always room for the saxophone and more modern performers. This led to 'end of the line' visits from the south. I remember the Don Rendell Quintet with Graham Bond on alto. Then Tubby Hayes mesmerised us with his technique. The Dankworth Orchestra with Dudley Moore on keys and Bobby Breen's vocal on 'Route 66' came to the Beach Ballroom, with the famous 'bounce' of its sprung dance floor, and even Ken Mackintosh brought his band up north.

The Amazing Alex Sutherland (2nd left) with vocalist Marisha Addison, Bill Kemp, Johnny Hartley and Laurie Hamilton at a Grampian TV session. Laurie was the guitarist I accompanied to the session in Perth

Miss Jeannie Lambe, the 'Highland Peggy Lee'

More surprisingly, Alex Sutherland (trombone, vibes and accordion) brought his amazing aggregation down from the Two Red Shoes Ballroom in Elgin. I remember standing agog as his lady vocalist, one Jeannie Lambe, (un)dressed to kill, performed her Peggy Lee numbers.

Not to be out-done, local pianist Munce Angus formed his big band; Cliff Hardie (still active in the south) led the trombone section. This was the first time I was introduced to 'inked' arrangements resulting in the sound of a proper 'big band'.

The Munce Angus Big Band (c.1962). The back row includes Johnny Hartley (bass), and Munce at the piano. 'Big' and 'Young' Ronnie are on trumpets in the middle row, along with Cliff Hardie and Alan Gall on trombones. The front row includes me on 2nd alto and Dave Milne on 1st tenor

A Sunday evening Jazz Club opened in a local school hall which became *the* place to go. In preparation for this, we became *bona fide* 'travellers' – exploiting a loophole in the then Scottish Sunday drinking ban. Piling into a car, complete with portable battery-operated record player and the latest jazz releases, we made our way up Royal Deeside. Stopping off at the Banchory Lodge Hotel, we would set up the player by the river to enjoy the sounds. On the stroke of 4pm we would repair to the hotel lounge where we ordered and consumed afternoon tea. Thus, qualified as bona fide 'travellers', the bar was opened, and we drank enough to set ourselves up for the evening jazz session – not *too* much of course.

We even entered the sextet in the Elgin Jazz Festival where I suffered the ignominy of not being rated at all in the tenor sax category: my early inspirational, but uncontrolled Coltrane-like noises finding no favour with any of the judges. No change there! Worst of all I had persuaded the lovely Patricia Thompson to join me for the day. Her sympathetic cooing only served to increase my angst. My manhood had been severely undermined.

Becoming more ambitious I formed an eight-piece band, the 'Big 8', featuring original works by James Grant Kellas, a lecturer in history at Aberdeen University. James had recently returned to Scotland from a spell at London University where he had led a unique band comprising five saxophones and three rhythm. He had even played at Ronnie Scott's club in its earliest days in a set of gigs organised by pianist and fellow student, Michael Garrick, under the title 'Jazz Goes to Kollidge'. Six tracks by the band recorded at the University of London Students Union in 1960 appear on the Garrick 'Kronos' album issued by Hep. I also penned a number of West Coast style charts. The band debuted at the Aberdeen Beach Ballroom on Friday 22nd November 1963, a date indelibly ingrained in the mind as the day of President John F. Kennedy's assassination in Dallas, Texas!

The Jim Philip Big Eight: Neil Simpson (above) on drums. (To the right) Alan Gall (trombone), me (tenor), 'Swanee' Mackenzie (trumpet), Johnny Brechin (guitar) and Johnny Hartley (bass)

By this time, I was well aware of most, if not all, of the musicians plying their trade in and around Aberdeen. We had the beautiful *art deco* Beach Ballroom, the Palais de Dance and most recently the Palace Ballroom, just off Bridge Street. All had dance bands and from time to time I would be called in for a dep. When we got to hear of 'ad hoc' weekend sessions centred on the County Hotel at Perth, guitarist Laurie Hamilton, from the Beach Ballroom, and myself decided to give it a go. A drummer from Perth, Bill Kemp, would ensure a rhythm section. That Sunday night we had Jim Mullen on bass, yes, *that* Jim Mullen, up from Glasgow. From Dundee we had sax players Malcolm Duncan and Roger Ball, soon to emerge as 'The Average White Band'. The session went far into the night – a foretaste of what it would be like 'down south'.

***

With my 5-year apprenticeship as a Chartered Accountant of Scotland complete it was time to turn my thoughts to the future. How would I continue to develop my playing? The answer lay in an advert which appeared in the local paper inviting suitably qualified people to apply to Brighton College of Technology for something then titled as 'Numerical Methods', which subsequently morphed into the more recognisable 'Computer Science'.

Having spent a holiday with my parents in London, I knew that there was a fast-non-stop train between London and Brighton, 'The Brighton Belle'. Here was a way to get to the London Jazz Scene. Dad was pretty forward thinking and agreed that computing might be a particularly useful addition to my accounting qualification. He saw that I was itchy and would not settle for a 'brass plate' on a wall in Queens Road – Aberdeen's professional row. Following an interview, I was offered a place on the College's first intake.

In September 1964 it was off to Aberdeen's Joint Station for the journey south. Clutching my beloved Selmer MKVI tenor sax, record player, my 'Desert Island Discs' collection of vinyl – mainly the latest Miles, not to mention some clothes and my father's emergency supply of blankets, I got on the train. It was quite the longest I had ever seen. My father looked up and down the platform at what he considered to be the 'Flower of Scotland' leaving the 'Homeland'. There was a slight moistening of eyes, appropriate to the occasion. The whistle blew and the steam train shuddered into motion. I was off and would never return permanently. The cliché is … 'and the rest is history'. My father, God bless him, voted Scottish Nationalist from that day on. Who can blame him?

***

CHAPTER II

Cutting My Teeth

I arrived at Brighton College of Technology in September 1964 and found it full of civil and mechanical engineers and a very oppressed General Studies Department. Nevertheless, I formed a small wind group and worked hard at improving my flute playing. There was a lively scene in Brighton with a big band led by Geoff Reynolds employing a number of excellent south coast players. I also got some deps with the Sid Dean Band at the Mecca Complex and some work with small groups.

Most of my time was spent on the 'Brighton Belle' travelling to 'Town' to seek out like-minds around the jazz pubs. I earned the reputation of being the 'Mad Scot' who came all the way from Brighton to the Market Tavern, up York Way in Kings Cross, to play in rehearsal bands. For the first time I found that the style I was striving for gained some acceptance.

I joined Graham Collier's 12-piece band, a band led by Barrie Forgie (later to become leader of the BBC Big Band) and played some deps with the young band of the late Pat Evans. He was a particularly interesting case. Around the same time, he worked with Bill Ashton and Mike Kershaw to assemble the London Schools Jazz Orchestra. This of course morphed into the now countrywide National Youth Jazz Orchestra (NYJO). Bill Ashton took over the leadership and remained as its guiding light until 2009 when he moved 'upstairs to become Life President. I clearly remember that my only contact with Bill, who was known as 'King of the gigs', came when he fixed me for a commercial gig in the West End, quite a different scene!

If you had mentioned big bands in the 1960s, what would spring to mind – Basie, Kenton, Ellington? Barrie and Graham's bands had all the classic charts and it was a great learning experience to play in the style of 'The Atomic Mr Basie' or Stan Kenton's 'College Series' and 'Adventures in Jazz'. Aside from 'Take the 'A' Train' or 'Satin Doll', Ellington was more difficult to find. After all, his writing was often aimed at a specialist soloist *viz* Johnny Hodges, Harry Carney, Cootie Williams, or Ray Nance.

Following in their footsteps came Woody Herman, the 'cool' West Coasters and later Maynard Ferguson and Buddy Rich. If you delved further back in time you encountered the trombone of Tommy Dorsey and ace clarinet players Benny Goodman and Artie Shaw. Glenn Miller was out of the question for the ambitious artist! On the other hand, Barrie and Graham used their bands to test their own compositions and arrangements and **that's** what made the experience **so** exciting.

Also, Morley College in Waterloo ran rehearsal bands on a Saturday led by trumpet player Gordon Rose. We could pit our wits against the advanced, if heavy sounds of Bill Russo. Russo, a significant Stan Kenton sideman and composer/arranger, had formed a London band, including Gordon in the trumpet section, which recorded his music. We younger guys got the benefit of playing the charts.

This lifestyle – full-time study in Brighton, living on £7.00 per week (including travel) and travelling up and down to Town three times a week, took its toll. My weight fell below ten stone and I began to shake a bit. I learned the hard way, that one could not survive on mental drive alone. I was diagnosed by a local doctor as suffering from a mild form of vitamin deficiency! I eased back and decided to take a job in London, programming 3rd Generation Computers.

***

I said goodbye to the Brighton College of Technology on the 3rd January 1966. It had been a mixed experience. The maths largely defeated me as I had a gap of five years since 'Highers' (the Scottish equivalent of A' Levels, but with more subjects to take). On the other hand, as the most qualified Chartered Accountant on the course, I was giving the lectures on accountancy. What's more, the money was running short. I had long since vowed not to punish my father any further with respect to funding.

At the start of all this, I discovered that the hitherto enlightened Scottish Education Department would not recognise any funding for my situation. My five-year struggles in an accounting office at £2.00 per week disqualified me from any funding for further education. I even found myself stamping up and down the offices in the Aberdeen Education Department. And yet, it had been much publicised that the country was in desperate need of new technology skills. Though I presented myself as an outstanding candidate for such support, it was to no avail. I would not qualify as a mature student until I reached the age of thirty. I couldn't wait *that* long!

Management Dynamics (MD) in West London, close to Heathrow airport, was more appreciative of my potential. Initially funded by Brooke Bond, of tea fame, the company had set itself up as computer business applications service centre. 3rd Generation computer installations occupied an entire floor of the building and at that time could only be afforded by the largest of corporations. I found myself a position in the Applications Development Department in the build of applications and associated support for the client base. It all started with running company payrolls but developed into systems for accounting, stock control and financial management.

Bright implementers, often from the best universities, wiped me out with such speed of implementation that I nearly lost my job. No matter, the 'turkey came home to roost' when their programs often failed under pressure, causing much customer dissatisfaction. My laboured approach seemed to produce a more solid product. To this day, clever people with a vision, often underestimate the tiresome need for the specification and implementation of exception conditions.

I finally won my spurs when Sheepbridge Engineering, a customer in the Midlands, contracted for the provision of a payroll system. This was to be based on the in-house MD system, but reduced in size to fit their smaller computer with, of course, the delivery of application variations! As I was recognised as being the most qualified analyst, I was assigned the tasks of 'Specification, Systems Architecture and Implementation' and given two of the brightest graduates to help with the coding. We were a great team. We delivered on time and the testing went smoothly with customer acceptance not a problem. Later I was summoned by the MD management and told that the company had made its *first* profit on such a task.

***

Living in Richmond, West London and working near Heathrow, made access to my love for music much easier than my previous thrice-weekly commute from Brighton. I read the now sadly departed *Melody Maker* from cover to cover each week to see where **it** was all happening and who **it** was happening with.

This resulted one evening in my still under-nourished self, sitting next to Barbara Thompson, the saxophone and flute player, in one of the rehearsal bands. She immediately recognised my plight. We struck a bargain; I would do the driving, but when I picked her up from her family home in Wimbledon, she would feed me. Many Shepherds Pies later I was more or less back on the charge. Barbara was aware that at that time I was striving with the flute and having been 'properly' trained at the Royal College of Music, she did her best for me

Bobby Breen

John Marshall

I struck a similar deal with Johnny Dankworth's blues singer, Bobby Breen. I would do the driving and in return he would let me back him ('Route 66' and all that …) around the pubs and clubs. I met a number of sidemen in this way, including the marvellous drummer, 'mover and shaker', John Marshall.

More importantly, on the 28th October 1966 I met Nina, the lovely lady from Sweden, at the Gatehouse pub in Highgate when I parked my tenor sax case under the table she occupied; she still puts up with me to this day.

I talked to John Marshall about my idea for a five-piece band. I wanted to move away from the focus that most local jazz 'heavies' used in those days; mainly blues and thirty-two bar 'standards' where each member soloed, challenging each other, and exchanging fours. I sought to emulate the much more open contemporary approach of Miles Davis/Charles Lloyd and thus, the concept for my '5' was born. I hired the upstairs room at the Market Tavern and invited three other kindred spirits, Dave Holdsworth on trumpet and flugelhorn, pianist Mike McNaught and Chris Laurence on bass, to join John and I to try out our sketch arrangements.

Dave Holdsworth at the top of the steps to Ronnie Scott's 'Old Place', Gerrard Street c.1967

Dave had started his musical life on cornet and risen through the Yorkshire ranks of various brass bands before discovering jazz. Like me, he was a semi-professional, though earning his daily bread in college teaching and management.

Mike McNaught was a musician with the 'X' factor that set him apart from other musicians; a 'properly' trained musician having studied at the Royal Scottish Academy of Music (now the Royal Conservatoire of Scotland) in Glasgow. I could feel the 'magic' in his hands when he backed me. 16- year-old Chris Laurence was already making his mark on the scene as a member of the London Schools Jazz Orchestra, soon to morph into the National Youth Jazz Orchestra under the direction of Bill Ashton. But where could we present ourselves?

Melody Maker classified ad for 11th February 1967

Drummer John Stevens of 'free form' persuasion was plying his 'free' jazz trade with his Spontaneous Music Ensemble in the Little Theatre Club near Trafalgar Square. If we could supply a doorman, we could 'cut our teeth' midweek. Talk about devotion. I can't remember how many staircases we had to haul up the drum kit to reach the room! It was a miracle that any audience was able to find us at all!

Ronnie Scott & Tubby Hayes – The Jazz Couriers c. 1959

So far, so good! And then John Marshall focused his remarkable powers of persuasion on manager, John Jack, to let us have a blow at Ronnie Scott's 'Old Place'.

Ronnie Scott's original Jazz Club opened on the 30th October 1959 in London's Soho at 39, Gerrard Street. Its mission: somewhere to play and to hear, **the MUSIC.** Descending a steep iron staircase, through the entrance and along a narrow passage, the club opened out into a veritable 'dive bar'. The lighting was subdued to say the least, hiding its state of disrepair.

Over the years, Ronnie and his business partner Pete King, overcame all manner of obstacles to bring the greatest luminaries of the jazz art to the club. To ply one's trade on its 'hallowed' stage became, and remains, the ultimate ambition of every aspiring jazz musician.

Ronnie's soon became a niche magnate for visitors to the City. The audience demand grew, such that Ronnie and Pete seized the moment in 1967 and engineered a move to more spacious premises at 47, Frith Street. But what of Gerrard Street, it still had 18 months to run on the lease? A moment of inspiration; Ronnie and Pete appointed Soho 'wise man', Doug Rouse, to keep it open as the 'Old Place' for the 'young jazz kids'. Doug's tenure was short-lived and the management passed to the indomitable John Jack.

Not much (sorry, no) money was spent on the environment, but there was always a beer or whisky available to accompany the barest of micro food offerings – I can't remember much wine in those days!

The Mike Westbrook Sextet c.1966 (From left to right): Harry Miller, Malcolm Griffiths, Alan Jackson, Mike Westbrook, John Surman, Mike Osborne. They would 'dress down' for the Old Place

Jazz 'kids' arrived from all parts. An invasion from the South West brought Mike Westbrook and his following from Plymouth and beyond, with names such as John Surman and Mike Osborne to give the atmosphere lift off. Westbrook offered jazz stability with everything from a sextet to a big band, while the aforesaid sidemen attracted others to compete for playing – *nae*, jousting time. Our own session with the Jim Philip Five went well and being more organised than the average outfit, John Jack was persuaded that we could reliably occupy a slot on the marathon Saturday 'All Nighters' (12-hours of jazz for just 10 shillings!). Charles Lloyd's 'Sombrero Sam' was always called for. Also, George Russell's 'Honesty' from his 'EZZ-thetic' album had been scored for the band by Dave Holdsworth and that was popular too. We were in!

This was the age of the Hammond organ and the Old Place had one in spades. We often shared the 'All Nighter' bill with Bob Stuckey on the mighty Hammond. Supported by Phil Lee or Terry Smith on guitar with John Marshall or Martin Hart on drums, he blew the place apart. For added excitement, Dudu Pukwana, on alto sax from South Africa, often joined the set and wow!

The Bob Stuckey Quartet (from left to right): John Marshall, Dudu Pukwana, Phil Lee and Bob Stuckey at the mighty Hammond organ

From time to time, visiting musicians from across the 'pond' might sit in. When the Buddy Rich band was playing at Frith Street, sidemen like alto man Ernie Watts would pop in and enjoy the freedom of a blow at the Old Place. Also, sax man Dave Liebman, once a pupil of Charles Lloyd and later a member of the Elvin Jones' and Miles Davis' bands, sat in with my quintet on his first trip to Europe.

Mid-week was the time when everyone available dropped in to test their mettle. I remember John Marshall's flat mate, bass man Dave Holland played to such effect that Miles Davis, no less, persuaded him to fly away and join him in the States. John woke up to find a note on the kitchen table, 'Gone to the States for Miles! Dave'. We shall never know what happened to the ROVER 75 car that Dave left parked outside John's flat when he took his bass to Heathrow? Guitar maestro John Mclaughlin would sit in from time to time before he disappeared to America and look what happened to him!

* * *

One of the most significant benefits that the Old Place had to offer was 'Big Band Monday'. Everyone looks for the jazz blower and rhythm player to get an opportunity to stretch out, but what was there for the jazz arranger and composer? Big Band Monday.

Mike Westbrook and his band, featuring John Surman and Mike Osborne, pioneered these evenings, an idea modelled on the Monday sessions at the Village Vanguard in New York's Greenwich Village. *Inter alia*, Graham Collier, Mike Gibbs, John Warren, Chris MacGregor, recently arrived from South African and leader of the Blue Notes, and the New Jazz Orchestra, all took the opportunity to feature their charts. These band leaders would select their line-up from the guys they heard at the club. A Sunday rehearsal would be called and on we went the next evening.

I was flattered when Graham Collier called me to front-up on a chart he titled 'Aberdeen Angus'! I was encouraged to give it all my wind on the tenor. Playing for Chris MacGregor was an unforgettable experience. He gathered us all together for a rehearsal at the Old Place one Sunday in mid-1967 before we set off for Birmingham, on what I believe was the band's first gig out of Town. Can you believe the line-up? Dave Holdsworth, Mongezi Feza trumpets; Mike Gibbs, Malcolm Griffiths, John Mumford trombones; Dudu Pukwana, Mike Osborne, Ronnie Beer, me and John Surman reeds; Chris McGregor piano; Dave Holland bass; Alan Jackson drums

We travelled to Birmingham by coach amid a curiously scented 'haze' emanating from the back seats. Chris conducted from his portable piano at the front of the coach, dressed for the part in traditional flowing robes. His arrangements were more in the way of detached themes and riffs, relying on the feel and spontaneity of the band members to convey the message.

Naturally, altoist Dudu and pocket trumpet man Mongezi were familiar with the themes and flexible structures of Chris' music and led the way as we did our best to simulate the spirit of the 'townships'. John Surman would jump in, often with Mike Osborne closely on his tail. I remember trombonist Malcolm Griffiths waving his horn. In short, the Mike Westbrook contingent were well to the fore. I confess that I, for example, felt the mood a 'wild shout' rather than a 'skirl'. That evening, our playing left the watching local Birmingham band, led by Johnny Patrick, bemused and doubtful.

It was never quite the same again. There was not a falling out as such, between the South African players and their British counterparts, as some people have suggested. It was just that *everyone* was in the line-up – an embarrassment of riches, I'd say.

Johnny Dyani and Louis Moholo were in Denmark at the time of the Birmingham gig. When they joined the band, upon their arrival in England, all Chris' 'old buddies' were together. This nucleus of South African players, augmented by some 'free' thinking Brits, begat the 'Brotherhood of Breath'. Surman, Osborne and Alan Skidmore did their sax thing, while Malcolm Griffiths and sometimes Paul Rutherford provided their brass interjections. We shouldn't forget bass man, Harry Miller, who became a regular member of the

'Brotherhood' and other great players like Harry Beckett, Evan Parker and Gary Windo, who were absolutely in their element.

* * *

The Old Place and its youthful players were well advertised in the *Melody Maker*, such that attendances grew, enabling John Jack to offer the acts some recompense for their efforts. It obviously did not pay enough to live on, but in its short life the Old Place became *the* place to play for the up-and-coming jazzers. Attendances varied of course. The weekend 'All Nighter' attracted those who had nowhere else to go. A section of the audience would even last the entire night, only struggling up to depart when the tube trains had once again opened up.

The Melody Maker 'Bill of fare' for Ronnie's May 1967. A small prize will be awarded to anyone who can spot the Jimmy Philip Quintet in the line up

My Five always enjoyed the solid support of Nina and Nell, Dave Holdsworth's partner. Sipping a lager 'shandy' they must have heard the same 'licks' a hundred times over, but their endurance never wavered.

Nina and I, **The Happy Couple'**, spliced the 'main brace' on Friday 9th June 1967 at Mortlake Registry Office in the company of a select gathering, comprising John Marshall, Best Man, Toril Madsen, Bridesmaid. Musician, Dave Morse, took the pictures and we all enjoyed Nina's now legendary Swedish 'open sandwiches' in our flat in East Twickenham.

Of course, the next day was the Old Place 'All Nighter' and this could **not** be missed! Our set finished at midnight and hastily packing everything away, Nina and I piled into my Triumph Herald for the trip to Aberdeen to celebrate with my parents and family.

In those days, all signs pointed the way to 'Hatfield and the North'. Needless to say, I was more than drowsy after the gig and had barely reached Apex Corner when I gave in and parked the car for a shuteye. Thus 'refreshed', I pointed the car north up the A1.

The honeymoon, up to Aberdeen, thence through Inverness to the Highlands and Islands, allowed time for reflection. We had not booked ahead and we found my chosen hotels already fully booked. Before panic set in we found a cottage up a hillside which showed 'Vacancies'. Maybe not 'Brigadoon' but it would serve the purpose.

We were last down for breakfast and had to suffer the *knowing* glances of the other travellers as we squeezed into the breakfast room! Whereupon the lady of the house threw open the door to present us with the largest cauldron of steaming porridge (salt not sugar) you could imagine. Nina was handed the spurtle and our married life started on the right foot as she had to serve all the guests. Being a Norwegian/Swede, it was a tough ask, but she quickly learned the ropes.

* * *

Melody Maker classified ad for the Bull's Head, February 4th 1967

My recollection is that 'establishment jazzers' paid not a lot of attention to what was happening in the Old Place. Ronnie himself was busy getting Frith Street up and running, so both he, and manager Pete King, had plenty on their plate.

Tubby Hayes was as busy as ever and had gained some recognition across the 'pond', while top professional, Bill Le Sage, was active with people like Dick Morrissey at the Bull's Head and other surround establishments. In addition, the modern guys were getting work out of Town. The bottom line was that there was **no** money to be made at the Old Place!

It's probably true to say that the majority of the young guys were off on 'their own thing', often with their own combos and mostly with their personal arrangements and compositions. But pass marks would only be awarded by the 'jazz establishment' if the young jazzer could display some mastery of the jazz standards and BEBOP themes with their associated complex chordal sequences and lines. Charlie Parker ruled! The challenge was to get up on the stage along with the jazz establishment and demonstrate survival in battle formats of solos and fours.

***

I can recall being invited to Cambridge and the Footlights Club to front the local rhythm section. No one told me but they had also invited top tenor man Stan Robinson to share the stage. It started with a friendly blues, but Stan became somewhat needled when I gained a little more audience reaction than him. He suggested some titles with which I was not familiar. I somehow got by and yet again, unfairly gained audience response. Stan then proceeded to take-over and in an extended solo demonstrated who was boss. 'What can you do next?' he enquired. 'What about 'Stompin' at The Savoy'?' I spluttered. 'In Db,' he said and was off again. At the end, he recognised that he had taught me a lesson. But I had survived and the audience had enjoyed the evening. He was content with that.

Fast forward a year or two and I found myself on the stage at the world-famous London Palladium. The concert featured US star singer Johnny Mathis, backed by the Maynard Ferguson UK Orchestra, or, that's what was expected. By some chance, Maynard and his band were absent – on tour!

The string section was ready to go, but the brass and woodwinds made up a distinctly dep band. In the reeds, Stan Robinson was on the 1st tenor chair and doubles, with me on 2$^{nd.}$

Now, Stan was peerless on solo passages but distinctly slower in sight reading. Mathis had with him his own Musical Director to take us through the programme. We were OK on swing but on the ballads, Stan was badly caught out. In my experience, orchestral scoring of this type would, more often than not, allocate the wind sections to a specialist, perhaps the baritone player or the 2nd reed, leaving the tenors with the jazz. On this occasion, however, it was not the case. After two failed attempts, the MD came over and presented the reed ballad parts to me. Boy, was I glad to recall my days in the pit orchestra at Aberdeen's Her Majesty's Theatre. Where was the Brighton star Johnny Franchi, who could read and play *anything*, when we needed him? Somehow, I got through, though I needed a couple of pints before we took to the stage that evening.

* * *

My first rehearsal with the New Jazz Orchestra, 26th July 1966: (from left to right) Dave Gelly (tenor); Mike Gibbs (trombone); Dicke Heckstall-Smith (soprano, tenor sax, flute); George Smith (tuba); me (flute, tenor); Barbara Thompson (flute, alto); Neil Ardley (MD, conductor)

After a number of false starts, and names, the New Jazz Orchestra (NJO) finally emerged in 1964 at the Green Man, Blackheath in South East London. It started out as a rehearsal band for players and arrangers until composer and arranger Neil Ardley took over, to bring some organisation and method to the band. Barbara Thompson had found her way into the line-up. When the great multi-instrumentalist Don Rendell vacated the reed section to concentrate his efforts on the quintet he co-led with Ian Carr (also a member of the orchestra), Barbara suggested that I might like a trial for the place. I remember the event distinctly – 26th July 1966 – the night England beat Portugal 2:1 to qualify for the World Cup Final against West Germany at Wembley Stadium. In most big bands, at that time, you were regarded as a specialist saxophone player – alto, tenor or baritone. The NJO was quite different; you had to state your doubles. In this way the band listed its reed section as Barbara Thompson (flute, soprano, alto, baritone), Dave Gelly (tenor, clarinet, bass clarinet), me (tenor, flute, clarinet) and by no means last, Dick Heckstall-Smith (tenor, soprano), sometimes doing his Roland Kirk 'double-horn' trick and playing both at the same time.

All this enabled Neil Ardley to table charts *a la* Gil Evans with Miles. It's only a slight exaggeration to say that with Ian Carr on flugelhorn you could close your eyes and imagine that you were there with Miles and Co. Mike Westbrook's wild jazz circus could, and still does, present a broad palette of sound, but ours was the only band to transport audiences into the wider fare and unique sound world inspired by Gil and Miles.

* * *

Perhaps the NJO's most definitive and collectable album is titled **Le Dejeuner Sur L'Herbe**. This was recorded in September 1968 and released in 1969 with Neil Ardley leading a fabulous line-up – Derek Watkins, Henry Lowther and Ian Carr on trumpets and flugelhorns; John Mumford, Mike Gibbs and Derek Wadsworth trombones; George Smith tuba; Barbara Thompson, Dave Gelly, Jim Philip and Dick Heckstall-Smith reeds; Frank Ricotti vibes; Jack Bruce bass and Jon Hiseman drums

Michael Garrick was pianist with the band for a time and in those days of my 'rave up' tenor solos, I was given his classic composition 'Dusk Fire' to get my teeth into. It is featured on 'Le Dejeuner Sur L'Herbe', but the version to savour was captured on a 'live' BBC 'Jazz Club' broadcast on the 28th June 1968. Humphrey Lyttelton set the scene with his introduction and I blew a storm, with a solo sandwiched between Barbara Thompson's flute and Frank Ricotti's vibes.

I really hit the spot with Alan Cohen's arrangement of John Coltrane's 'Naima'. *Jazz Journal* critic, Steve Voce reviewed the album very favourably in May 1969. It was a pleasure to observe that Steve did not get bogged down by the 'Gil Evans' only look-a-like tag and as did some others. In his article he wrote:

'And the best is yet to come. Alan Cohen's arrangement of Coltrane's *Naima* with its tenor solo by Jim Philip is the most exciting thing I've heard since Gil Evan's *Barbara Song*. I was so moved by this exquisite performance that I contacted Neil Ardley in London to find out if the atmospheric allusion to Evan's recording was deliberate. Briefly, Evans' score builds in a brooding intensity, which is suddenly lit by a more oblique entry from Wayne Shorter's tenor. This solo of Shorter's is to me one of the most prized moments in jazz. Shorter is a fine soloist when given his head, but here, tied by Evans' arrangement, he is quite untypical, and his beautiful solo takes on an unusual affinity with some of Getz's best work. The same thing happens with the NJO's *Naima*, with Philip and the band approximate the same atmosphere, except that Philip's allusions to Getz seem more overt. In construction the piece has nothing in common with Evans' *Barbara Song*, but the feeling is there.'

Also, this performance I feel, was largely responsible for me getting a vote for 'Talent Deserving of Wider Recognition' in the 1969 *Downbeat* Critics Poll.

The band's orchestration gave me space. If you think of the early Miles and then the 'Kind of Blue' transformation, that's exactly what the NJO offered. Many critics of the day entirely missed the platform it offered the soloist. **NO** other band offered me that.

We toured the UK college circuit supporting great names like Georgie Fame, Alan Price and the Animals, played with Eric Burdon at The Marquee, provided backings for Manfred Mann on several of his recordings and recorded jazz broadcasts for the BBC.

The New Jazz Orchestra in Concert: (from left to right) Unidentified, Derek Wadsworth, unidentified, Mike Gibbs (trombones);Neil Ardley (MD, conductor);Dick Heckstall-Smith (tenor); Dave Gelly (tenor, bass clarinet), me (flute, tenor), Barbara Thompson (flute, alto)

2008 saw the release of 'Camden 70'. This 'live' BBC Jazz Club performance was recorded on 26th May 1970 at the Jeanetta Cochrane Theatre, London as part of the Camden Jazz Festival and the first gig in a UK tour. Notwithstanding the difficulties of live performance, all the original 'Dejeuner' compositions, plus some bonus tracks, are reproduced in an exciting format, including my feature on 'Naima'. I feel here that somehow, I managed to take inspiration to a new level. This 'Naima', I suggest, is representative of what I call my 'analogue saxophone period', captured here in full flow. The album as a whole is a fine tribute to the guys in the band:

Director/Conductor/Arranger: Neil Ardley; Trumpets: Mike Davis, Nigel Carter, Harry Beckett, Henry Lowther; Trombones: Derek Wadsworth, Mike Gibbs, Robin Gardner; Tuba: Dick Hart; Reeds: Barbara Thompson, Dave Gelly, Dick Heckstall-Smith, Jim Philip; Keyboards: Dave Greenslade; Vibes and percussion: Frank Jellet; Guitar: Clem Clemson; Bass guitar: Tony Reeves; Drums: Jon Hiseman.

My erstwhile colleague, Dave Gelly, tenor saxophonist, writer, broadcaster and author of the sleeve notes for 'Camden 70', commented on my 'rather square demeanour' on the band photograph they chose to use on the album cover. When I looked more closely, I had to agree with his observation. Over the years I reconciled myself to the epitaph – 'unidentified tenor', a quote from a picture of the NJO Dick Heckstall-Smith used in his personal memoir, 'The Safest Place in the World'.

* * *

Whilst Neil Ardley was full of cool and jazz sophistication, in Jon Hiseman, a true leader and driving force on percussion, I recognised a business mind that could offer a living to sidemen. He was doing deps all around for the top rock bands of the day. To fulfil his dream, he took no time to form his own band – Colosseum. I had been on his shortlist, but I was not a 'rocker' at heart and Dick Heckstall-Smith filled the bill. Jon served up the 'Valentyne Suite' on his second album which included contributions from the NJO. Together, this aggregation played the Fairfield Halls, Croydon, Birmingham Town Hall, Lanchester Polytechnic, Coventry and the Queen Elizabeth Hall, thence to Portsmouth Guild Hall and Brighton Dome.

Jazz writer Ronald Adkins of *The Guardian* was on hand at Lanchester Polytechnic on 24th January 1970 to review a triple-bill – Colosseum, Jack

Bruce & Friends (Jack's new post-Cream band which was set to take off for a tour of the US) – and the New Jazz Orchestra:

> 'There is not much wrong with the youth of Britain today, at least not in Coventry. On Saturday night the Main Hall of Lanchester College saw thousands squatting shoulder-shoulder on the bare floor from where, in an atmosphere growing more stifling by the minute, they listened to four hours of music. No one grumbled, no one collapsed: they sat quietly while the music played and clapped and cheered when it stopped. As a veteran of FA cup ties and smoky jazz clubs who lurched out before the end for oxygen and a hot dog, I offer them my envious congratulations.
>
> They had come to hear the new Jack Bruce group, Jon Hiseman's Colosseum and the New Jazz Orchestra – in that order. It was Hiseman who gathered the widest applause. Both he and Bruce lead pop groups that show traces of jazz, while the NJO with Tony Reeves on bass-guitar blasting across all but the best-miked soloists, proved it could get over to a mainly pop audience. The hall's acoustics militated against the band's more refined moments, and the sensitive backgrounds to such numbers as 'Rebirth' and 'Naima' were badly distorted. Not that it mattered, especially with saxophonist Jim Philip playing so well on the latter.'

* * *

All the comings-and-goings in the early days suggested to some that Barbara and I might be something of an 'item'. Nothing was further from the truth. Jon sussed this out and moved in to make Barbara his lifetime partner. What a team they made! If anything, Barbara was the more progressive in terms of her music. While Jon was earning the 'bread', she worked steadily with her bands Jubiaba and later Paraphernalia, both at home, but more often in Europe. A look at Wikipedia finds her working closely with Andrew Lloyd Webber on his musicals *Cats* and *Starlight Express*, his *Requiem* and the classical-fusion album *Variations*. She has written several classical compositions, music for film and television and was a member of the United Jazz and Rock Ensemble, a 'star-studded' line up of international band leaders. She was awarded an MBE for her services to jazz in 1995

The onset of Parkinson's disease meant that Barbara had to give up active playing in 2001. Then, more tragically, Jon suffered a collapse with brain tumours in 2018. An operation failed to see him recover and he sadly passed away. There is no more to say!

Barbara and Jon – What a team they made!

* * *

Chapter III

And then came the tap on the shoulder ...

It was a case of 'wheels-within-wheels' as far as band line-ups were concerned in those days. Michael Garrick was pianist in the NJO for a time and also a member of the successful Don Rendell-Ian Carr Quintet. I depped for Don on one occasion and when Michael formed his sextet, he invited yours truly to join Art Themen and Henry Lowther in the front line. The wonderful Coleridge Goode was on bass and my good friend and 'Best Man', John Marshall, completed the band on drums.

Michael Garrick was a prolific composer both in the conventional jazz metier and in a quirky style of his own. He delved into Poetry and Jazz and developed a choral work called 'Jazz Praises'. It was first performed at St Michael the Archangel, Aldershot on 2nd November 1967 and subsequently toured the country. We even played at Queens Cross Kirk in Aberdeen and drew this comment in the *Aberdeen Press and Journal:*

> 'The idea of jazz in the Church of Scotland may seem incongruous – to some even sacrilegious – but Garrick's compositions are not just musically brilliant: they are also deeply religious in a moving and meaningful way.'

When we performed 'Jazz Praises' in St Paul's Cathedral on 25th October 1968, jazz writer Derek Jewell led his review in the next day's *Sunday Times* with the headline, **'Ferocity in Church'**.

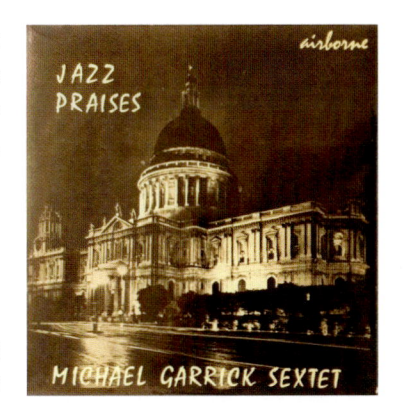

The album cover for 'Jazz Praises', recorded at St. Paul's Cathedral 25th October 1968

The Michael Garrick Sextet, Central Hall, Westminster, 12th April 1968 (from left to right) Shake Keane (trumpet, flugelhorn); Michael Garrick (organ), me (tenor).

Michael wrote 'Rustat's Grave Song', dedicated to the memory of his late friend, Rustat Hensted, and featured me as a Highland Piper on tenor! I shall never forget the skirl under the vast Dome of St Paul's. Mike had spent hours practicing late at night in the organ loft and had worked out the exact location of the pipes so that he could unleash them to their full dramatic effect with the original 'Surround Sound'! With Coleridge's help, Michael recorded the concert on a single microphone suspended from the gallery and released it as 'Jazz Praises at St Paul's Cathedral' on the Airborne label. When it was reissued in 2008 as a CD on Michael's Jazz Academy label, sleeve note writer, Dennis Harrison, noted that my 'swirling saxophone solo' anticipated the 'popular cathedral work of Jan Garbarek and John Surman in later decades'.

* * *

Normal jazz gigs saw us around London in venues such as the Old Place, the Phoenix, Cavendish Square, the Torrington, Finchley and the Green Man, Blackheath. We drove up and down the country on pre-motorway highways on the college and university circuit. Can you imagine the difficulties we had travelling in those days, especially heading 'Oop North'. The M6 is bad now but I remember the A6 as being even worse.

John Mundy, a student at Keele University in Staffordshire wrote some kind words after a gig at the Students Union on a foggy night in February 1968:

With the Michael Garrick Sextet. Trumpeter Henry Lowther is in the background

'Garrick himself was sufficiently relaxed to allow his tremendous sense of humour to break over the audience, but the main credit must go to the front line and to Jim Philip in particular. Moving up, down and around, and obviously becoming deeply involved in the session, Jimmy showed what a good musician he is. His clarinet solo on 'Rest', a derivation of an Indian raga, the sentimental flute in 'Little Girl', his imitation Webster tenor sax in 'Webster's Mood' and above all, the supreme melancholy of the fantastically haunting 'Rustat's Grave Song' made his efforts the force of the evening.'

* * *

The '*Melody Maker Jazz Scene '68*' concert at the Royal Festival Hall on 18th May 1968 saw the Sextet line-up as part of a veritable 'jazz bash'. We played alongside the Stan Tracey Big Band, the Alex Welsh Band, the Rendell-Carr Quintet, the Chris McGregor Sextet, vocalist Salena Jones and US guest stars Hank Mobley and Phil Woods. Mike again challenged all around on the 'house' organ (the first time it had ever been played at a jazz concert). It was a highlight for my parents, down from Aberdeen, as the only time they had ever heard me in action. Dad was totally bemused but assumed that it must be good if I was playing at such a famous venue. I think he was quite proud really.

Later in the year, on 23rd October, we played on another extravaganza; a George Wein '*Jazz Expo '68*' concert at the Odeon, Hammersmith featuring vibes stars Gary Burton and Red Norvo and Ronnie Scott's exciting Nine Piece Band. Writing in *Jazz Monthly*, Roger Cotterrell described our contribution as 'an imaginative set from six fine musicians'.

The Sextet made several broadcasts, including a BBC Radio 3 'Jazz in Britain' session recorded at Maida Vale studios on 10th October 1969. This was issued as 'Prelude to Heart Is A Lotus' by Gearbox Records in 2014 as a high-quality vinyl LP and CD.

Its release caused some consternation amongst reviewers as to who should be credited with the reed solos – Don Rendell or yours truly. I am only credited with flute on the album sleeve notes and so it was assumed that Don took the tenor *and* soprano solos which follow each other in quick succession on 'Sweet and Sugary Candy' or that perhaps a 'mystery' player had joined the session for that track.

Not so. It's certainly, Don on tenor. Who could match his brilliance! But I follow on my much-prized soprano – there's no doubting the personal sound. Whatever possessed me to later sell that instrument, I wonder? Nothing I've played since has ever matched its quality! I solo on flute on 'Heart Is A Lotus' and 'Little Girl', while Don takes the honours on 'Song by the Sea'. We join forces on clarinet for 'Webster's Mood'.

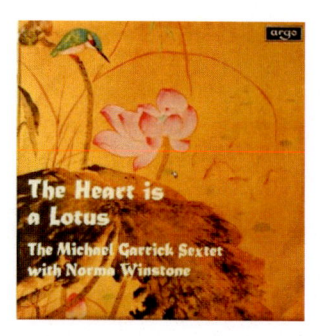

Norma Winstone augmented the Sextet when we recorded the 'Heart Is A Lotus' album for the Argo record label in January 1970. Her remarkable vocal qualities blended into the frontline as if she was a seventh instrument. I played on four tracks, recorded on the first of two sessions: 'Heart Is A Lotus', 'Beautiful Thing', 'Temple Dancer' and my tenor feature 'Rustat's Grave Song'.

The LP went on to sell about 1,500 copies – not bad for a British jazz record and has become a highly collectable item.

Michael was a gifted composer, but I couldn't help feeling that his charts were moving in a direction that taxed my limited technique. By then, I had joined the London Jazz Four and it was taking most of my time, so Michael and I agreed to part. Norma continued with the sextet as an instrumental voice, singing the parts I had played on tenor.

Nina and I went to Mike's funeral at the Amersham Crematorium in December 2011. Imagine my surprise when I heard the sound of my flute echoing round the hall. His son(s) had selected one of my tracks from 'Jazz Praises at St Paul's Cathedral' with the sextet to support the service. I can't have been so bad after all!

***

You will recall that I was introduced to the 'Jazz Big Band' sound by my two Aberdeen close football friends, Norman and Neil Simpson. It was through them that I discovered the exciting Maynard Ferguson and his various albums, like 'Messages from Newport'. Before forming his own band(s) Maynard, a Canadian, came to prominence as a high note trumpeter with the great Stan Kenton band in the late 1940s and early 1950s. I had immediately purchased LP copies and could be found singing the 'lines' to myself as I walked back to my office after lunch. I dreamt of playing the part of tenor man Carmen Leggio in 'Tag Team' – what an entry he makes!

Now, 'It came to pass', in the late 1960s that Maynard was to play in Town and that, at last, I had a chance to see him. By all accounts, he had got into some trouble in America and was banned from playing there, but being Canadian born and bred, he was able to use his 'British' passport to live and work here. He was backed by a UK band stacked with our top session guys, but no longer seemed able to hit his notes consistently and appeared to have lost his stratospheric best! I went home to Richmond a little deflated.

Maynard Ferguson, hitting the stratospheric heights

In no time at all, he was fronting a band on the twice-weekly broadcasts of Simon Dee's then very popular TV show, *Dee Time*. The band was stuffed with the hot guys based in the North West, like saxophonist Gary Cox. More importantly Maynard was now getting a regular blow and was able to get his lip in!

In between times, he put together a touring line-up and, with the help of Manchester-based trumpeter and fixer Ernie Garside, he was truly off and running. One evening during a rehearsal with the New Jazz Orchestra, I felt a tap on the shoulder. 'Could I be available for a gig with Maynard's road band?' I was asked. Of course, I said **'YES'**. Maynard had been a particular hero of mine, so you can imagine how exciting it was to be invited to sit in his sax section, even if the invitation came just as I had decided to return to my day-job in IT.

The gig was to be in Swansea on 9th October 1970 and I had an important client meeting that morning but, if I could make the Gunnersbury roundabout for 2pm, I could be picked up in the band bus.

Dressed in my 'client' best I must have looked a peculiar sight standing at the entry to the M4 for the inevitable late arrival of the bus. But there was more to come. We had to make a detour to pick up Maynard in Windsor. Was he ready for the road? Of course not. I can't remember exactly when we eventually set off for Swansea, but we were late, very late!

A phone call ahead helped a little, but when we arrived, we witnessed a packed hall being entertained by half a dozen or so of the guys who had made their way separately from Manchester. Maynard concocted a story about road work problems on the journey and suddenly we were hailed as heroes for getting there at all.

Not a good start for the sight-reading Jim P. No matter, lead alto man, Peter King, welcomed me warmly and quickly helped me to organise the pad. The band roared into life. I was on the 'Carmen Leggio chair'!

The next chart was to be a hot arrangement of 'Eli's Comin'', a hip modern song by Laura Nyro. Maynard took the microphone and announced that he would now feature a fine 'up-and-coming' tenor man, Jim Philip. I hastily scanned the chart but couldn't spot a solo being called for. 'What's he talking about?' I hissed to baritone man, Rod Watson. 'Don't worry son, you'll feel it,' was his laconic reply.

Maynard hit the downbeat and we were off. Fortunately, the arrangement transpired to be similar to a Bobby Lamb opus with which I was familiar; plenty of roaring introduction and chorus, then nothing. 'Stand up and blow-the-roof off Mr Tenor Man!' With eyes tightly shut I gave it my all. Thinking that I was soon to run out of ideas, I opened my eyes only to find Maynard urging me on! I ploughed on till finally the band was restored and I was able to sit down. Maynard insisted that the audience applaud my efforts. And they did!

When the concert was over and we were packing away our instruments, I was approached by an ardent Welshman. 'I have been waiting for this for twenty years,' he gasped. I realised that we had hit the spot and our late arrival was long forgotten.

My next gig as a dep with Maynard's band was at the 100 Club, Oxford Street; a 'home' venue with no frantic travelling to worry about. This time I was asked to take 'Willie Maiden's chair'. It proved to be bit tricky and my first encounter with Michael Abene's arrangement of 'Whisper Not' had me busking and chancing my arm. But it was a great experience and the fulfilment of a youthful dream. I wrote to Norman Simpson, my old friend in Aberdeen, with a report of what it had been like.

Maynard's UK band was by now fully established and its line-up buttoned down. Meanwhile, as I will soon relate, I was fully committed to a new role as a Project Manager in the IT industry. The demands of Rank Film Processing Laboratory's financial system held my full attention as I sought to bring them into the then modern 'Computer Age'.

***

There's a wonderful postscript to my time with Maynard's band.

Sometime later found me with some business colleagues having a late lunch in a local hostelry, The Ostrich, in Colnbrook, just off the A4. In by-gone days, The Ostrich was known as the first coaching inn out of London, a place where travellers would dismount having hopefully and safely traversed Hounslow Heath without an encounter with a highwayman; horses would be changed and ales supped. In more recent times it never failed to offer something truly special on its menu: a grilled Dover Sole, perhaps, and braised celery. Remember those days!

So, there we were. Lunch was over, but this was in the days when old business friends and colleagues would continue to sup and compare notes. As the afternoon wore on and glasses were emptied and refilled, conversation turned to what we might do next. 'Might the guys be up for something a little bit out of the ordinary?' I wondered. Maybe a trip to Hammersmith to see Ms Jacquie Byard might be on the cards? In those simple days Jacquie offered entertainment in the style of what today we might call the *exotic* dance. I found myself raising my voice and suggesting, 'Let's go and see Jacquie Byard!'

At this moment, a lady tapped me on the shoulder. 'Say young man, do you know Jaki Byard'? she challenged in an American drawl. My brain flipped into top gear. Surely, she couldn't be referring to the lady dancer. The only *other* Jaki Byard I knew was the US jazz piano player who featured on Maynard Ferguson's 'Newport Suite' album. 'Yes,' I said. 'He's a jazz piano man. He played with the trumpet man Maynard Ferguson. 'You know of Maynard?' she exclaimed. 'Yes, I replied. 'I've actually played for his band.'

With that, she took me by the hand and led me across the room. Yes, you've guessed it. There was Maynard at a table – she was Mrs Maynard! Of course, he couldn't recall my playing with his band on the Swansea gig, but was more than happy to engage in a chat.

I returned to our table and my dumbfounded friends. Ever the perfect gentleman, as Maynard got up to leave, he came over to say 'Hi', to the guys and then summoned the barman to buy us a round of drinks. You can't say better than that.

Thoughts of a visit to see the other Jacquie Byard were now long forgotten.

* * *

Bobby Lamb – trombonist, composer, arranger, teacher and band leader

Trombonist Bobby Lamb occasionally depped in the NJO, where I was given plenty of scope to do 'my thing' on numbers like 'Dusk Fire' or 'Naima'. One night he tapped me on the shoulder and, being the consummate diligent semi-professional, I duly accepted his summons and turned up to a late hour studio rehearsal in Soho. I found myself installed as a member of a big band newly formed by Bobby and fellow trombonist Ray Premru and sitting next to the wonderful and much-lamented tenor/reed man Duncan Lamont on 1st tenor. What a band! Over twenty pieces and brilliant writing from the two leaders. And why was *I* in it? I surmise that Bobby recognised something of the then contemporary jazz explorers in me which was not to be found in the major session players of the day.

Who is this Bobby Lamb I hear you say? Irish born from Cork, he arrived in England to play for Teddy Forster in 1952 and before long found himself in the trombone section of Jack Parnell's Big Band; the erstwhile star drummer for Ted Heath, led one of the top and well-connected outfits in the land.

However, Bobby's ambition showed no bounds. Off he went across the 'pond' to the States to study and catch up with the big band scene over there. And catch up he surely did. In no time, he found himself as a sideman touring with Charlie Barnet, Stan Kenton and Woody Herman. Returning to the UK he settled in with Cyril Stapleton's BBC Show Band supplemented by freelancing with various orchestras ranging from 'Top of the Pops' to Symphony Orchestras, both at home and abroad.

In later life, 1982, and in recognition of his studies and broad experience, he was appointed as Director of Jazz Studies at the Trinity College of Music in London. This offers a home to the growing population of young 'jazzers' seeking to formalise and round their experience to prepare them for the demands of this 'scary world'. Bobby continued his playing often on European tours supporting the likes of Frank Sinatra, Ella Fitzgerald and Peggy Lee; also touring with Buddy Rich in the 1970s.

The Lamb/Premru band I joined in 1970 was unique in featuring a four-piece French Horn section in addition to the conventional reeds, trumpets, trombones/tuba, plus a four piece-rhythm section. Perhaps there were echoes of Kenton here with his 'mellophonium' aggregation of the 1960s?

Recording for the BBC at Ronnie's in March 1971 saw the likes of Derek Healey, Gus Galbraith, Ronnie Hughes, Kenny Wheeler and Tony Fisher on trumpets, with Chris Pyne, David Horler, Jack Thirlwall, Ray Premru, Bobby Lamb and fellow Aberdonian Cliff Hardie on trombones; John Jenkins on tuba, and ex-Ted Heath man Ronnie Chamberlain and top 'jazzer' Alan Branscombe leading the reeds along with me, Tony Roberts and Ken Dryden; Steve Gray on piano, Arthur Watts on bass and the fabulous Kenny Clare on drums. Plus, the French horns of Nick Busch, Colin Humphrey, Tony Lucas, and John Pigneguy; and the percussion of John Dean.

At the Notre Dame Hall in May of that year, we had trumpet giants Greg Bowen, Derek Watkins blowing the roof off and Keith Christie soloing on trombone. This line up, playing compositions by Bobby and Ray, Steve Gray and Kenny Wheeler, produced a heavy sound which proved too much for one '*Jazz Journal*' reporter.

Later that year, we had a visit from the great Austrian pianist Friedrich Gulda for a concert at the Queen Elizabeth Hall. Gulda had started out in his native Austria taking all the honours before him in the classics. He made his debut at New York's Carnegie Hall at the age of twenty and even had the temerity to reject the award of the 'Vienna Beethoven Ring' in 1969 as he turned to jazz for 'nourishment'.

In the mid-1960s he had produced an album for CBS entitled 'From Vienna with Jazz'. He had written a three-movement concerto for piano and jazz orchestra and scoured the length-and-breadth of Europe for *emigre* US jazzers whom he deemed good enough to play 'his' music. He even flew Mel Lewis over from New York to play drums. This was the music he brought with him for the London concert.

Needless to say, one look at the score confirmed that we were in for a challenge, but as the parts had been issued beforehand, I felt confident that I would make it OK. Arriving at the afternoon rehearsal in my usual good time, who should I bump into but Friedrich Gulda himself. He regaled me with his comments relating to the scarcity of good jazz music performers on the continent and that he was glad to be in London.

I was then presented with a surprise challenge; 1st tenor/reed man Duncan Lamont couldn't make the rehearsal and would I play the flute parts as scored? Help! Well, one look at the parts signalled that this called for a 'proper' flautist. Harmonic fingering was the only way to navigate some passages. Suffice to say I gave it my best shot. Fortunately, Duncan arrived in good time and between us we got by.

* * *

The band recorded only one more album, another live session, taped at the Queen Elizabeth Hall on 5th December 1971 and issued by Parlophone as 'Conversations'. Jazz writer Steve Voce has written at length about the concert in *Jazz Journal* (October 2018). Suffice to say that a huge audience, including a veritable 'Who's Who' of drummers and percussionists, paid tribute to the late Frank King, a fine drummer himself and writer for *Crescendo* magazine. By some trick of magic, the organisers had pulled together the 'mega star' triumvirate of Buddy Rich, Louie Bellson and our own Kenny Clare, to front the band. I can be heard briefly, together with tenor man Duncan Lamont on 'Cuchulainn', in the wake of Buddy's near-ten-minute tsunami of sound drum solo. It's hard to believe, but Buddy had real trouble with the tempo and Bobby Lamb had to face away from the audience and beat him in with his fist on his chest.

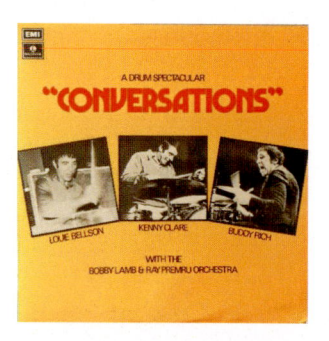

Bobby Lamb conducts the drum spectacular with Louie Bellson, Kenny Clare and Buddy Rich paying tribute to the late Frank King, Queen Elizabeth Hall, 5th December 1971. I am tucked away on the far left adjacent to the curtain. A mic stand points to my head.

In a band exclusively comprised of session players, with me as the sole 'free-spirit', 'all-star deps' inevitably needed to be called upon for live gigs. On one such outing at the Shaw Theatre, I encountered the *ultimate* challenge of a fast tempo joust with none other than Britain's greatest tenor player, Tubby Hayes. This brought the gig to an exhilarating close.

We met again at the open-air Holland Park Theatre on an occasion when Tubby was, recovering from massive heart surgery. At the interval, whilst most of us made a dash for the pub outside the park gate, it was noticeable that Tubby took a long-time to join us. Indeed, a cab had to be called to get him back to the stand! Nonetheless, we commenced the second set without more ado.

Then came 'Cuchulainn', the climactic Bobby Lamb flag waver, dedicated to a legendary Irish hell-raiser! I readied myself! The band stopped and off Tubby went at the obligatory high speed with me as usual hanging desperately to his 'note-tails'. All seemed well with this out-of-tempo frenzy until I suddenly heard Tubby desperately wheezing and gasping for breath. This increased until he stopped playing altogether, though his gasping continued.

In those days, we 'young lads' often engaged in high-speed outings followed by a meandering out-of-tempo song to the heavens. Instinctively, I fell off the tempo and, with horn lifted to the gods, proceeded to wail with conviction. Then, as if by a miracle, Tubby Hayes came again to life and off he went at the same high tempo, with me restored to the chase. This, however, was not to last. Once again, he gasped and stopped and once again, I fell back on my out-of-tempo soliloquy. What happened next? Yes, you've guessed it; Tubby regained his breath and we were off again. This happened **three** times.

Of course, the audience was completely unaware of Tubby's situation. The people assumed that these tempo interactions were all part of the show and what a show it was!

The great Tubby Hayes (post-operation) – I clung to his 'note tails'

Not long after, Tubby returned to hospital for surgery to repair his leaking heart. As we all know, Tubby died on the operating table at the tragically early age of thirty-eight. What a loss! In the couple of times we played together, we probably didn't exchange more than half-a-dozen words, such was my respect for his reputation. That night, when it fell upon me to save the day, I felt as close as I ever had been to a fellow player.

***

My final date with the Bobby Lamb/Ray Premru Orchestra was a 'live' BBC 'Jazz Club' session from Sussex University in February 1972. It always revives a mixture of good and bad memories for me. Following Humphrey Lyttelton's inimitable introduction, I initially rose to the occasion and set loose on my featured number, Kenny Wheeler's gorgeous 'Ballad Sweet Ballad'. But as the open solo moved on, to my horror, I realised that I had lost track and wondered, with mounting desperation, how I might find my way back to the arrangement as laid down. My solo quietly went to sleep. Sensing my impending breakdown, the wonderful Kenny Clare let loose on the 'skins' and saved the day.

The next day I telephoned Ray and offered my resignation from the band. I realised that I was out of my depth. Ray, being the gracious gentleman he was, accepted my wish.

Nearly fifty years later I found out from jazz writer Steve Voce that my demise had been captured on tape and transferred to a CD-R! I placed the disc on my BOSE with some trepidation to discover that my initial efforts were not wholly out of place. To the outside listener there is little, if anything, of my disquiet. All seems in order and the band continues on. Did I overreact? Perhaps, but I remain to this day convinced that the demands of this fine band were beyond me.

Chapter IV

A Change of Direction

We now need to turn the clock back to 1968. I was beginning to feel that my '5' was running out of steam. We had started on a high, held the residency at the Old Place, successfully auditioned for the BBC and survived a live BBC Jazz Club broadcast. In those days, a fiver discreetly handed to a BBC sound engineer would result in a pristine reel-to-reel copy of the broadcast. It was strictly against the rules but the only way to preserve music that would otherwise be lost to eternity. Hence, an outing for 'Sombrero Sam' from 1967 on a compilation CD of my 'greatest hits' titled 'A Younger Man's Jazz', that my good friend John Snow and I put together in 2007.

There were some great times, but too often we seemed content to simply repeat our message. My sidemen were getting calls from all directions. John Marshall was drumming for everyone and his main thrust would mature eventually into Nucleus with Ian Carr and the Soft Machine. Dave Holdsworth, always the man to stretch out seeking new directions in the 'free' school, became a brass sideman with Mike Westbrook. Young Chris Laurence, by this time almost old enough to legally enter a public house, was on constant call. He enjoyed a fabulous family pedigree and could also be found playing his heart out in the 'serious' music orchestras.

Our pianist Mike McNaught, meanwhile, besides playing in my '5' and pursuing other musical activities also led his own London Jazz Four – a popular fringe-jazz group echoing the vibes/piano/bass/drums line-up of the Modern Jazz Quartet. Mike was seeking a concert outlet as a player/arranger and was market modelling his group on the lines of the MJQ and Dave Brubeck in an attempt to attract a broader audience and even make a sensible living from his talents.

The London Jazz Four c.1967: Back row (left to right) Mike McNaught, Len Clarke; Front Row (left to right) Ron Forbes, Brian Moore

The band appeared on BBC TV's 'Late Night Line Up' and the highly popular 'Michael Aspel Show'. They supported the Brubeck Quartet on its 1967 tour, drawing these words of praise from Dave's bassist Eugene Wright, 'I have seen them grow musically so I'm proud of them. Watch for them to appear in person because this group are going places.'

Mike's cleverly arranged album of Beatles tunes, 'Take Another Look at the Beatles', had sold quite well for Polydor, but the group's vibes player, Ron Forbes, then in the army, was due to be posted to Germany!

Young, vibes and percussion starlet Frank Ricotti might have been the answer but he was still busy learning his trade with Chris Laurence in their quartet. Also, he might have found the style of the LJ4 a trifle restricting at that time. The end result was that Mike asked me to join and be featured on flute. This led to the 'new' LJ4.

* * *

Before you could say 'Jack Robinson' I found myself in the CBS studios, along with Mike, Brian Moore and latest discovery Mike Travis on drums, recording 'Scarborough Fair', one of the most popular numbers in the band's repertoire and an entire album of jazzed-up Tudor themes. With a nod towards pianist Bill Evans, we even gave an airing to Henry VIII's original theme, 'Green Grows the Holly'.

With a natural appeal to the 'soft-jazz' market 'An Elizabethan Song Book' raised some encouraging reviews, especially across the provinces – in the days when the regional press took an interest in jazz and could influence people to visit their local record shop or come to a live gig.

Jazz Journal's Derrick Stewart-Baxter added his seal of approval with these words:

> 'This music is in fact far more virile than that of the MJQ. The spirit of the songs is never lost, nor is the gentle beat; Jim Philip's flute is exactly right ... McNaught's piano is fascinating, always darting here and there, backing Philip's splendidly ... the really outstanding track is the beautiful 'Scarborough Fair'.'

Nonetheless, he cautioned, 'I hope that next time CBS will let Mike McNaught do an album of his own choosing; the London Four have a lot to offer ...'

It was then that virtuoso bass man from Cambridge University, Daryl Runswick, joined the band. He arrived from the John Bird-Ian Curtis Quintet in a virtual swap for Brian Moore. Daryl already knew our driving drummer Mike Travis from playing together in pianist Reg Powell's trio at the Pickwick Club, where they had backed people like Jon Hendricks in cabaret.

We quickly built up a repertoire of pieces often drawn from popular material of the day. These, as in my '5', moved away from the standard jazz format of 'chorus, solos, fours and out-chorus'. The set list typically included Harry Nilsson's 'Without Her', 'Things We said Today', 'Fool on the Hill' by Lennon and McCartney, and Glen Campbell's 'By the Time I Get to Phoenix'.

Mike and I agreed that this library was too 'soft' for the Old Place. Our style was more suited to bars and clubs in and around London. We signed with bassist/agent/promoter Ed Faultless and were doing up to four gigs a week. We enjoyed quite a following in venues like the Hopbine, Wembley run by tenor star Tommy Whittle; the Torrington, Finchley; the Phoenix in Cavendish Square; the Palm Court, Richmond; out of Town clubs in Redhill, Brighton and Swindon; the wonderfully titled 'Joustings' in Hornchurch and even the 'hard core' jazz audience of the Bull's Head, Barnes.

> Playing at Finchley's Torrington, the quartet features the fragile, beautiful yet exciting amplified flute of Jim Philip showcased against the flexible, yet tightly knit rhythm section of Mike McNaught piano, Darryl Runswick - the best 'unknown' bassist in Britain, and drummer Mike Travis. **Alan Walsh, Melody Maker**

> The London Jazz Four, the modern jazz combo I predict most likely to succeed in 1969 and become Britain's biggest jazz attraction … **Jeff Rigby, Brighton & Hove Herald**

> 'This group are going places.' **Eugene Wright, bassist Dave Brubeck Quartet**

> A record I have enjoyed like no other in months comes from a jazz quartet who call themselves the London LJ IV and have managed to turn eleven sixteenth-century songs into the evocation of that age and this on Elizabethan Songbook. **Bradford Telegraph**

A Change of Direction

It won't sound the same again.

Great jazz never does.

The London Jazz Four would like to introduce you to their music.

Mike McNaught, piano, electric piano; Jim Philip, flute, tenor sax, soprano sax; Daryl Runswick, bass, bass guitar; Mike Travis, drums;

Alan Walsh's lengthy article for *Melody Maker*, the 'Bible' of British popular music, which appeared on 28 June 1969 reflected the growing interest in the band:

> "**IT WON'T** sound the same again, Great jazz never does," exhorts the stark black and white publicity poster. It may sound immodest to sing one's own praises but the London Jazz Four – who send out the posters in advance to every club that books them – have the talent and originality to back up their boasts.
>
> In five months on the tortuous jazz circuit, the group are achieving what many people feel is nigh on impossible: they are attracting a new audience to the music.
>
> How? By promotion of the group's name, by presenting their music as a pre-arranged programme, by trying to 'sell' the music to the audience and getting them involved – and most important by drawing their music from a wide variety of musical sources.
>
> "We may seem to be a very flexible group," said Jim Philip, who prefers the semi-pro jazz life at the moment, because his daytime job in computers gives him the freedom he requires, "and we are. But the music is disciplined and every number is an integrated production in an overall programme.
>
> 'We are basically working towards the concert idea. We expect and work at the audience listening to us and we don't aim to play for dancing, although much of what we play is danceable."
>
> *The London Jazz Four – an artist's impression*
>
> To preserve this sense of co-operation, Jim has deliberately avoided playing tenor or soprano sax with the group so far, although they feel now that they have reached the point where they could experiment slightly with new instruments.
>
> "We are trying to communicate with as many people as we can," said Mike McNaught, the band's leader and pianist. "If we can get someone to hear us by publicity then when he's in the club he hears something he can identify with – like a Beatle's tune – he'll listen to other things. And we've got him …"
>
> The London Jazz Four are four musicians with integrity and ability presenting refreshingly original music which is adding something to the multi-faceted face of jazz.

Mike was also interviewed by Jeff Rigby on BBC Radio Brighton and used the opportunity to announce the 'world premiere' of his new musical 'Blood Orange', in which the London Jazz Four would provide the accompanying music. I recall that it wasn't quite the spectacular event that Mike gave listeners to believe; rather an adjunct to his teaching work at the Rose Bruford College of Speech and Drama that served as an audition piece for students. I remember playing in the cramped orchestra pit of the Arts Theatre in Central London for a dress rehearsal and a one-off performance to a specially invited audience of 'important' people who appraised the talent performing on stage. The Brighton interview also gave rise to a rumour that we had recorded an LP with the great American vocalist Jon Hendricks and were anticipating a tour of America. Pipe dreams!

Even so, Mike was forever searching for new sounds and projects. He made a test recording of his take on some 'hits' of the day plus some of his own originals. He added trumpeter Henry Lowther, Chris Taylor on alto flute, Frank Ricotti on marimba and a string section to the LJ4 line-up. It was never released, but one track, 'Homeward Bound', found its way to YouTube in 2012. The sound is far from perfect, but it gives an idea of the direction in which Mike was travelling.

Mike McNaught – pianist, composer, arranger, teacher at home in his studio

* * *

When the LJ4 followed the Moody Blues, then at a peak of their popularity, on stage at the Reading University Graduation Ball in July 1969, we soon found to our cost that the flute alone could be constraining. We succeeded in all but emptying the Hall – a very salutary experience!

We had to react and expanded our sound palette with the addition of tenor and soprano saxes and electric piano. Daryl added the bass guitar to his considerable talents on the string instrument and we felt that we were 'in the van' with the incorporation of electronics. We continued to favour the Beatles, Jim Webb and Harry Nilsson as the basis for our material, contemporary pieces which could be reconstructed to enhance our jazz journey. Mike, and sometimes Daryl, would enrich 'show stopping' pieces like 'McArthur Park', and later 'Rosecrans Boulevard' to offer a jazz experience which was still (we hoped) recognisable to a broader audience. George Harrison's 'Something' received an almost Coltrane-like redefinition. This enabled us to broaden our repertoire and hopefully our appeal. We benefited greatly from the enthusiastic support of that late, great human being, Humphrey Lyttleton, compere of BBC Radio 2 'Jazz Club' for which we made several highly successful broadcasts.

* * *

Never one to rest on my laurels, I knew of the 'upstairs' room at Ronnie's Frith Street Club, which continued the spirit of the Old Place as a venue where new groups played to entertain and provide a more modest cost sampler for the jazz audiences. I would fire off a brief 'sales' note to Pete King each week in the hope that he would give us some consideration.

Then it happened! One Thursday, a group let Pete down at the last moment. What could he do? 'Why not call Jim Philip, he's been pestering me for months!' Quick as a flash I assembled the guys and we were on, playing the celebrated Ronnie Scott Jazz Club; the *ultimate* accolade for any UK jazzer!!! We gave it our best shot. We were tuneful, organised and so well received that Pete followed up with further 'short-notice' calls.

The Melody Maker announces the LJ4 support slot opposite Roland Kirk at Ronnie's, January 1970

On the next occasion, he called on us to do 'our thing' on the *main* stage of Frith Street, opposite of all people, 'Thelonious Monk'! It was a one-off and, truthfully, I can't recall much about the evening; but we were **there!**

In the last week of January 1970, Pete called yet again; this time to feature us opposite the mighty Rahsaan Roland Kirk and his wild multi-sax show.

The critics were out in force and most found favour with us. 'The London Jazz Four,' wrote the *Daily Telegraph* on 2nd February 1970, 'whose hybrid Jazz/Pop could win a major following in this country, showed at Ronnie Scott's Club that their appeal is to those who regard the electronic age as a blessing rather than a bane'.

In another report I was likened unto a, 'Wayne Shorter with a strong atonal approach and some outstanding soprano work'.

We were strongly influenced by the American group the Fifth Dimension and adapted their interpretation of the 'Magic Garden Suite', based on three themes by Jim Webb, as the opener to our second set at Ronnie's. We set the mood with a 'borrowing' from 'In A Silent Way', Miles Davis' mind-bending venture into electronics with our 'old friend' Dave Holland on bass.

Richard Williams, a rising star in the world of music journalism, with a keen ear for what was happening across the scene, picked up on this in his *Melody Maker* review of February 7th:

> 'The London Jazz Four is a very worthy band. Its members work hard to make music which is both attractive and thoughtful, and their new extended work 'Magic Garden Suite' is a case in point.
>
> The group managed to communicate its frequently understated message to a high percentage of the audience. Jim Philip was particularly impressive on soprano, tenor and flute, but I felt one particularly passionate tenor solo (late-Coltrane with touches of affecting Aylerish whinnying) would have made more impact if the rhythm section had followed him instead of staying in a four-square rock configuration.
>
> The night I heard them; Mike McNaught was using his new electric piano for the first time. He used it aptly, his note-clusters being a little funkier than those of the fashionable Hancock/Corea school. Daryl Runswick's bass was brought into the front line to state one lovely theme in tandem with Philip's tenor, and Mike Travis is an astute drummer, subtle in his use of tonal colourations.'

On that same evening, I clearly recall emerging from a solo and looking down to see none other than super-star tenor man Stan Getz looking up at me from the floor. All I can say here is that I felt that I could see Stan more clearly than he could see me!

* * *

My main role with the LJ4 was to develop a sound business model to build on the group's modest success. I conjectured that we should assemble a team comprising respectively, investment from myself, a sound-recording contract and a management-sales-media-booking team. If we each invested an agreed sum, we would be collectively motivated to work for success and therefore payback. Sounds simple!

We were approached by John Steel and Chas Chandler (sadly no longer), formerly the drummer and bass guitarist of the Animals, who were now scouting for talent. Chas was the man credited with discovering Jimi Hendrix. John was particularly enthusiastic about our ideas for an album. We proposed that the first side would comprise material by Lennon & McCartney and the second to Jim Webb etc. An advance was agreed, further investment discussed, and studio time arranged. Two demo sessions were set up at Studio 51 near Leicester Square.

John came to the first session and was so impressed by the demo that he laid out his ideas for university/college and festival gigs i.e., a 'soft rock' circuit – just what the doctor ordered! It was around this time that one of our most earnest fans suggested the name Atlantic Bridge to replace the moniker London Jazz Four. We had long debated the marketing merits of dispensing with the JAZZ tag and felt that the new name might aid our cross-ocean ambitions.

To our surprise, Johnny Gunnell, the younger brother of the 'characterful' circuit booker Rik, whose agency boasted strong connections with the powerful Robert Stigwood, came along to the second session with Chas. He took me on one side and said, 'You've got plenty of creative talent and it might take some months to get the act fully together.' There was a pause and then he uttered the fateful words, *'But life's too short.'*

'What do you mean exactly?' I asked. He spelt it out; he promised to review the output from the booked recording sessions, but he could not go ahead with the 'agreed' contract terms and declined my offer of recording for session fees only. Knowing that **he** would possess all rights to what we put down and with **NO** assurance of album release, I took the momentous decision to call the whole thing off. Johnny was not best pleased – it was once alleged that he threatened to 'rearrange' Georgie Fame's fingers when Georgie tried to switch management agencies! We packed our gear and left Studio 51. For a moment I feared for my life.

* * *

Not long afterwards, PYE records launched the Dawn label to seek out and feature 'new' talent which did not easily fit into existing defined categories. It might just provide the outlet we were looking for following the demise of the deal with John and Chas.

I was invited to meet Dawn producer Barry Murray early one morning immediately after the Whitsun Bank Holiday of 1970. Our conversation was suddenly interrupted by a phone call from one of his hitherto little-known acts – Mungo Jerry. The band had caused a sensation over the previous weekend at the Hollywood Music Festival at Madeley Heath, Staffordshire and stolen the show from 'super-groups' Traffic, Black Sabbath and the Grateful Dead and were calling in to report their 'break-through'. Hot on the heels of this call, Barry took others from the BBC and ITV requesting the group's presence on the two hottest pop shows of the day, 'Top of the Pops' and 'Ready Steady Go'.

Barry had struck gold – **Mungo Mania** took hold of the country and in no time at all, *'In the Summertime'*, rose to #1 in the charts. It was the UK's best-selling single of the year and it all happened in front of my very own eyes.

Barry was in raptures. He offered us a generous contract with an advance and return on sales. Unfortunately, as it turned out, we were never able to achieve a contract with a management and booking agency to complete the picture. Nevertheless, the recording went ahead over the 2nd to the 5th of June 1970 at the Pye Marble Arch studios, using the latest in multi-track tape-based recording available at that time.

There were six tracks: George Harrison's 'Something', 'Dear Prudence' by Lennon & McCartney, the Mike McNaught original 'Childhood Room (Exit Waltz)', and the three titles by Jim Webb – 'Dreams' and 'Rosencrans Boulevard', which formed the 'Magic Garden Suite' and 'MacArthur Park'. Mike and Daryl took advantage of the facilities to 'enhance' the end product with orchestrated passages which were incorporated and overlaid in the final 'mix'.

All overdubs were played by the band members. Indeed, 'McArthur Park' was completely transformed from the hitherto live performance structure. Also, it was now possible to lay down solos which were skilfully edited-in by engineer Howard Barrow, who was a great source of advice in the process.

The lavishly produced **Atlantic Bridge** gatefold album received mixed reviews in the jazz press as falling between two stools. The pop guys were similarly confused as to what it was. However, writing in the *Daily Mail* 9th December 1970, such issues mattered not to James Greenwood:

> 'High on my list for the best disc of the year is this lovely record by the young group that used to be known as the London Jazz Four (Mike McNaught – piano; Jim Philip-woodwind; Daryl Runswick – bass; Mike Travis – drums).
>
> Theirs is a very modern music but so structured that no one can have any difficulty in coming immediately to grips with its copious invention.

Atlantic Bridge -
'We are trying to bridge the gap between Pop and Jazz,' **Jim Philip**

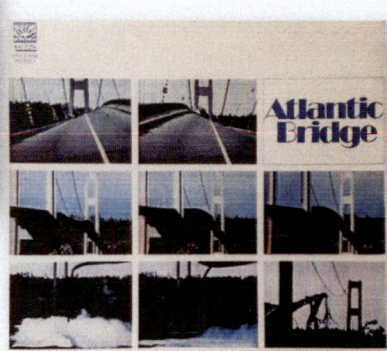

Bands, like bridges, rarely become airborne. When it happens it's hair-raising. Listen to this band, this Bridge, straining at its moorings: and forget gravity. Heaviness has nothing to do with it. **Press release December 1970**

High on my list for the best disc of the year is this lovely record ... no one can have any difficulty in coming immediately to grips with its copious invention.
Daily Mail 9th December 1970

Listen to Runswick's double bass or Philip's romantic improvising on tenor sax (using phrasing rather than tone to convey all his feelings). Listen only to the opening version of McArthur Park.'

However, it was not all plain sailing. *Melody Maker's* Richard Williams, who had written so positively about our appearance in support of Rahsaan Roland Kirk at Ronnie's earlier in the year, now performed a complete *volte face* with this offering:

'Philip's playing on this track (Rosecrans Blvd) is typical of what he does throughout the album going "out" for no reason when it would make more sense to play the pretty tunes. It's too forced and he's too good a player to waste his energy like this.'

Richard Williams does recover himself by the end of the review, but his words were of small comfort. 'Maybe I've been a bit hard on the album,' he admitted. Too late I felt. He had at that time dealt a mortal blow to our commercial aspirations.

* * *

Looking ahead, we had realised that in order to reproduce the 'album' effect, we would need someone to synchronise backing tapes to our live performances – it wouldn't be enough for us to desperately try and replicate the backing tracks by 'singing', especially not in some of the rough 'rock' basements and pubs we were playing at the time. Today the technology is readily available and it can easily be done, but it was pioneering then. Al Hyland, a friend from my hometown of Aberdeen, was eager to get involved and take that side of things forward, but without the crucial management contract in place to publicise the band and organise gigs, I could not envisage ever being able to 'feed' the band's families.

My head dropped. I had also awoken to the fact that my fellow players were mostly seeing different optional paths for themselves. The commitment to my then IDEAL for the **Atlantic Bridge** resided only with myself. Whereas, I had turned fully-pro to make a go of the LJ4 as it morphed into **Atlantic Bridge**, the other members of the band came under pressure from fresh opportunities.

The entire rhythm section made the 'Child Song' album with trumpeter Henry Lowther; a move which I felt compromised our identity. Mike was also getting calls to arrange and MD for many popular artists. Daryl, meanwhile, became a top sideman and song writer for people of the stature of Cleo Laine. I recall that our final gig was at a famous pub on the corner of the Seven Sisters'

Road. We didn't officially disband Atlantic Bridge; we simply couldn't find a way of obtaining the crucial support, funding and paid work for the enhanced line up!

* * *

Being the ultimate semi-professional, I decided I had achieved all that I could; it was as if we had reached the final in our own Olympic Games, but just failed at the tape. I had enjoyed most of it but recognised that I did not have the all-round competence to pursue a life as a successful professional session man. Yes, I would continue with the gigs as an eager sideman, but the dream was over.

As it happened, my erstwhile IT systems house Management Dynamics had just discovered the need for something called IT Project Management. I was offered a senior position with the company. This demanded all my time. I put my musical instruments to one side.

* * *

Chapter V

'There comes a time in life which has to be taken at the FLOOD' – the Bard.

Now it was back to the Day Job. I took up my post as Project Manager at Management Dynamics Software Services in February 1972. What did this, then freshly minted title, actually mean, I hear you ask. You could say that I was rather like the ringmaster of a circus, coordinating and directing a multitude of dynamic forces – business application, technical solution, with personnel and financial constraints. This was the emerging world of IT that I naively entered. The risks were great and a mere hair's breadth in interpretation of Requirements Specification might separate success from failure, but oh my, that final round of applause could be a joy to savour, *if* you got it right.

***

I was soon put to the test at a sales meeting to secure a deal with Rank Film Laboratories at Denham. The company's business system, largely run upon punch card tabs and collators, simply could not keep up with the booming film industry, so they had decided to purchase an ICL (International Computers Limited) 1901 tape-based computer. Management Dynamics had the technical expertise in place to support the project, but they needed someone who understood the business objectives and deemed me to be the man for the job.

But first we had to settle the deal. Rank had already recruited an IT systems analyst and he led the meeting. Jim Downer, an older guy, hitherto in charge of the existing Rank service, sat quietly in the corner. Though he was recognised as the guy who *understood* the business, surely, the need was for someone who understood the new technology – a common fallacy?

We won the job. Management Dynamics offered me a good deal and I was back.

It goes without saying that the job outcome was probably one of the best I ever achieved and my close relationship with Jim Downer proved to be the key to the project's success. That's not to say that all was plain sailing. We had a moment of panic 'at the death' when the computer controls registered a mismatch as the sales ledger statement-run went live. Thankfully, a midnight investigation proved that the statements were OK. Jim could release his statements and Rank would be paid.

We enjoyed an after-hours whisky by way of celebration. I had helped to solidify Jim's pension with Rank, who even offered me a job, but I decided to push on with Management Dynamics.

* * *

Over time, users became more demanding with respect to IT/computer support for their businesses.

The Singer Sewing Machine company had 175 retail stores in the US and many in Europe. Therefore, for stores with a wide product range, stock control and up-to-date information was critical to cash flow and profits. The company required a system that could connect several tills together in each store and act as a central point for the collection of real time information and invited the industry to respond.

IBM and NCR, the 'monsters' of the day, declined an offer to bid and only Friden Inc. in Oakland, California, accepted the challenge. However, in a major drive of commitment, Singer *bought* Friden and the result was the 'Singer System 10' – a proper business computer able to support and onward process 'Point of Sales' requirements.

'There comes a time in life which has to be taken at the FLOOD' – the Bard.

In the UK, what could have been more traditional than **Young's Brewery?** Based in the heart of Wandsworth on London's South Circular Road, here was a company transporting all of its local product by Shire Horse and embracing nothing less than a farmyard as a Head Office. Yet it became a pioneer in IT business support.

Young's purchased a Singer System 10 and chose Management Dynamics to implement the requirement with yours truly in charge. One of the benefits of the Singer System 10 was that the architecture and technology deployed was such that even *I* could understand it. The implementation proceeded to time and budget.

One special feature of the project was that staff morale was always fully supported by an invitation to the 'Sample Room' at the end of each day. Of course, this was always under strict supervision and upon arrival a member of Youngs' staff would brief us on the history of each keg as a prelude to the **sup**.

One evening the rain was teeming down and we laughingly made a dash across the already flooding farmyard to the Sample Room. We didn't mind if the rain delayed our journeys home if there was beer to sample. The downpour continued and we soon became in danger of being marooned. Our Young's host leapt into action to affect a rescue. He had a pair of substantial Wellingtons and set off to the security gate to obtain boots for us all. I remember a photo being taken as we made our escape, embarrassingly clutching our expensive leathers and covering our smart business suits.

It was a small price to pay for the installation of the Singer System 10, which more than proved its worth to the brewery. The system was so successful in the IT market that ICL later took over Singer Business Machines; a move that with further technical developments, ended in the eventual release of the world beating ICL ME29.

***

Situated close to the Tate Gallery on Millbank, the now defunct CCTA (Central Computer and Telecommunications Agency) – the Government quality and standards body, afforded the IT business community with regular business discussions and forums which I attended as part of my senior role in Management Dynamics. It gave me the opportunity to meet and converse with owners and senior managers in the emerging IT Services market.

Alan (later Sir Alan) Thomas, MD of Data Logic

One such meeting, sometime in 1977 as I recall, led me to meet Alan Thomas, the Managing Director of the then youthful Data Logic. We discovered a common interest in music including jazz. Indeed, although at that time Alan could barely sight read a note from the page, he was an accomplished piano player; one of those people who could enter a room, sit down at the piano and entertain the gathered throng until the barman shouted, 'Last orders, please!' Being a single note 'woodwind man' myself, how I envied this ability.

After-hours talks revealed that Alan had assembled a tight-knit management group comprising no more than half a dozen working shareholders, each of whom had a clearly defined role. He was growing the business and had persuaded a couple of top technical 'whiz kids' to join and thereby enhance his company capability profile. He also needed to hire some senior management people to control and help direct the business.

Not long afterwards I found myself attending a 'final' interview session at his then home in Baker's Wood, Denham. This was not too far my own residence in Osterley Park.

Alan's delightful spouse Angela settled me down with a friendly coffee. Of course, Alan was on the phone. I awaited with bated breath. Not for Alan one of these modern aptitude tests. He placed a disc on his state-of-the-art music system and the room filled with the sound of a very contemporary styled tenor sax player. 'Who's that playing?' he tested me. I did not recognise the sound. How could I respond? Alan had told me that Data Logic had an arms-length sister company in Norway. Could there be a link to Norway? I knew of only one Norwegian saxophonist. 'Why that's Jan Garbarek,' I asserted hopefully. Jan was not that well known in the UK at that time, and I had hit the spot. The interview was over and the offer would be in the post.

***

The success of the Data Logic I joined, lay in its management structure and the experience and qualities of the executives who staffed it. All had relevant knowledge and experience of the emerging IT industry, with the additional advantage that each had a specific skill to deploy *viz* strategy, sales, technical know-how, administration or financial. They each knew their boundaries, but above all, they worked together as a 'team'.

Bill Barrow, or 'Uncle Bill' as he was known, was in charge of administration. His primary function was that of personnel. Dipping into his bottom left-hand desk drawer, he could be relied upon to pull out a staff member's up-to-date CV. With a twinkle in his eye he could tell us how we were doing. His industry knowledge enabled him to readily process joiner candidates submitted for screening, for by this time the industry recognised skill(s) sets *viz* Project Manager, Systems Analyst, Technical Specialist or Programmer. In addition, he maintained regular contact with the relevant colleges in the recruitment of graduate trainees.

Needless to say, I and most of the other senior team were out and about all week but we always felt in touch. How was this achieved?

Each Friday, at about 4pm, MD Alan Thomas held 'open house' in his Greenford office. We were all welcome and we could help ourselves to a glass from his open cupboard. I clearly remember my first such session. The meeting was in full flow as I entered. Some of the longer serving guys were waxing lyrical about their projects and it all sounded very sophisticated and involved.

At an appropriate moment, Alan held up his hand and introduced me. 'This is our newcomer Scot, Jim Philip,' he announced. 'Jim, now that you have been here for a week, how do you feel and what have you achieved?'

I was able to tell the gathering, that on *that* very day, I had sold two Graduate Programers for a year each. Not maybe, the most dynamic of claims but Alan showed his class by reminding everyone that such deals provided the 'bottom line' to underpin more financially risky high-tech projects.

Compared with 'Big Company', methods all this had me persuaded that I had done the right thing by joining Alan's team. I found myself expounding on this to Irishman, Allan Wood, one of Alan's founder co-directors. 'I have looked under all the stones and can't find fault with any of it,' I claimed. How wrong was I to be? It was only a matter of months till Alan and his fellow shareholders sold the company to Raytheon, the American communications and military giant.

Despite my chagrin, there was a lot of synergy in this deal; *inter alia* Raytheon, in addition to its well-published war systems, was into Air Traffic Control, comprising radar, and green VDU terminals linked to a massive UNIVAC computer mainframe. They had also purchased Cossor Electronics based in Harlow, Essex, which was similarly into Air Traffic Control in the UK. Data Logic was strong in technical systems development and possessed an up-to-date technical capability and strong technical management, while Lexitron, another acquisition, could now offer the 'world of commerce' one of the first civil office-based word processing systems. Thus, Raytheon Europe was born and guess what? Before long, Alan Thomas became *President* of this new entity.

***

By the late 1970s, organisations beyond the business world, especially the police, were looking at the potential of computers to improve their systems. It was at this time that a 'man', subsequently titled the 'Yorkshire Ripper', was plying his dire and dark trade throughout the North of England. Data Logic, partnered with Data General, won a ground breaking contract with the potential to transform the 'baddie' seeking and capturing capability of the South Yorkshire Police Force, headquartered at the wonderfully named Snig Hill in Sheffield.

There were two main applications. First, the system would be used to provide details of previous convictions for use by the courts. Secondly, in an operational role, it would provide a search of records of convicted persons and identify possible suspects from descriptive information received from witnesses. Moreover, remote sites in the county could be fully connected without compromising the inherent constraints in the Official Secrets Act *vis-à-vis* access. That was the easy bit!

Working within public sector contractual constraints could often hamper the well-intentioned systems houses and end user with equal force in the 'fixed price' implementation phase. Requirement variations would be uncovered and a deal of valuable time taken up discussing and agreeing these. You can imagine that the team from South Yorkshire Police were past masters in arguing their case! It behoves me to praise Data Logic's project manager, John M. Smith, who 'got the job done' without too much bloodshed.

Ironically the 'Ripper' was apprehended by the good old Vehicle Registration system.

I, of course, now taken 'at the flood', banged on the Home Office door calling for the system to be replicated across the 50 or so Local Police Authorities. 'Crime and the criminal do not stop at these artificial boundaries,' I thundered when I addressed senior police officers at the Police Staff College, Bramshill in Hampshire. I pushed my case, but to no avail. I sat alone at lunch!

Last thought. There was a 'good guy' on the police team at Snig Hill – a guy who would be in charge of the delivered system and stood alone as someone who understood what he needed to do the job. Today I see his name on the punishment list for Hillsborough. Reading between the lines, I surmise that once again, he was only trying to rectify the blunders of others.

***

In stark contrast to the gloomy shadow of argument, depression and terminal decline cast by traditional British industries in the 1970s, the IT/computer industry was burgeoning and Data Logic was no exception. The Raytheon acquisition had opened new markets and Data Logic was prospering in the City financial arena. At the same time, technological advances had opened further opportunities for solution innovation.

Bell Laboratories on the USA's East Coast had spec'd and developed the transistor. Valve technology was declared redundant and all at once the inexpensive portable radio was available to all. Bright guys on the American West Coast grasped the meaning and by the end of the 1950s the Integrated Circuit was developed and patented by Texas Instruments. Years of miniaturisation followed, eventually leading to the 'microprocessor' which opened the door to the brains and competitive innovators in Silicon Valley. All at once such leviathans as IBM (International Business Machines) and NCR (International Cash Register) were to be severely challenged.

In the UK, I noticed that in the early days of 3rd generation computing, a number of young 'lads' with aptitude, side-stepped the university route and plunged straight into this new IT services world as speedy developers. Why not! Over £1K year from the off was better than theoretical plod.

In the van was one such bright spark, Michael J. Bevan.

Though he had initially prepared for university entrance, two years of National Service in the Royal Air Force gave him a taste for earning and on demobilization he joined the then Ministry of Works. Here he met an ICT 1301 mainframe and, thus encouraged, became an indispensable software developer. Little standard computing capability was supplied in those days and Mike soon developed a reputation as an 'ace'. This was recognised by ICT itself and soon he joined that organisation in its laboratories as a principal engineer.

Michael J. Bevan

Having got to grips with the architecture and innards of the 'computer', Mike set off on his own to establish a name for himself in the computer services industry. Not content with mere 'sales and purchase ledgers', he sought 'gold' through the development of industry-specific and administration-application packages and their portability across several computers. These forays did much to establish Mike's name throughout the UK services industry such that, when the UK Software Houses Association was conceived, Mike was elected its Chairman.

Furthermore, Mike Bevan, in effect became a 'visionary' associate of Data Logic's Alan Thomas. Up to speed on all the Silicon Valley developments, Mike had conceived and was developing XIBUS, an advanced ring-based secure, micro-processor computer. Alan Thomas, however, felt that this innovation did not sit conveniently within either the Data Logic or Raytheon structures.

It was agreed that *pro tem* Mike would set up Micro Logic within the Data Logic structure. This took off with special feature micro hardware/software solutions being developed to meet specific company requirements.

Bevan was now at full bore and it soon became clear that nothing would deter him from chasing his dream. Before long, with seed-corn investment support from a couple of the original Data Logic shareholders, Xionics Limited was established.

He was fortunate to be joined by Ian Richardson, one of Data Logic's top network systems designers and discussions were engaged to fund the development of XIBUS – the intelligent 'guts' of Bevan's vision.

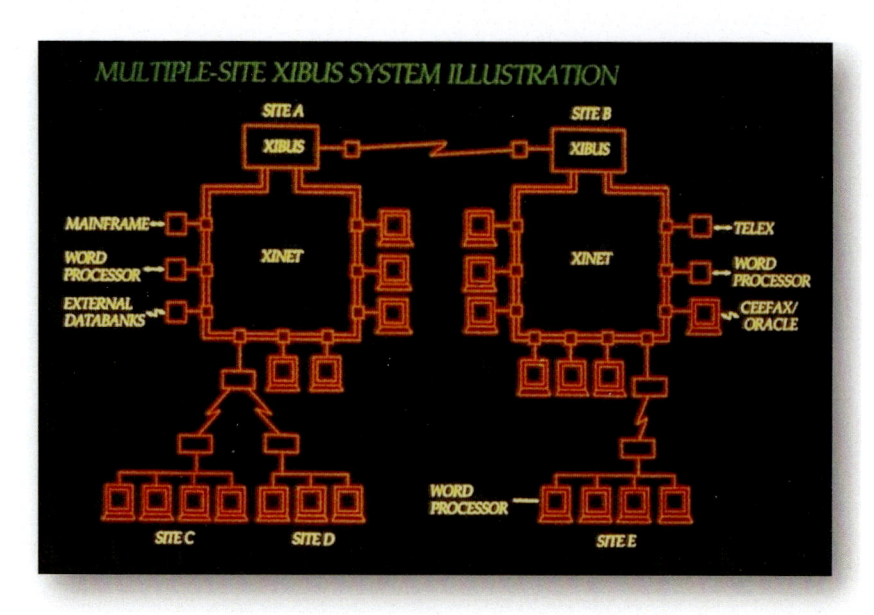

The revolutionary XIBUS Multi-Site Computer Architecture

After these many years, it is not easy in a few words to condense Mike Bevan's business solution into a simple Management Summary. Suffice to say that his philosophy encompassed *all* that is currently accepted as the 'norm' in today's business environment; the development of a multi-function Workstation. In other words, a *Personal Computer* or *PC*, with shared resources, gateways, and of course a network topology. Moreover, not content with theoretical concepts, Mike embarked upon a programme of computer and software development to offer the 'networked business office user' its *ultimate* work platform, both text and voice. Xionics, he believed, 'should always respond to the requirements of the user, for technology *per se* was valueless unless it could be harnessed to specific business needs.'

Such was his passion and persuasion that his approach to BP Oil enlisted some financial backing and other, then household names, soon followed suit: Calor Gas, Scottish Gas, Allied Breweries, Littlewoods, and ICI. Xionics would supply systems to improve their productivity.

These early beginnings proceeded much according to plan. Xionics' principles of open architectures (which made upgrading much simpler), local area networks and integrated office systems were soon established and with such success that Rolls Royce and the Midland Bank soon acquired a 25% stake in the company.

With this support in place, in July 1980, the company under the direction of fellow director, Phil Dickinson, established low volume manufacturing activity in Letchworth, Herts to standardise the build of the XIBUS controller. Most importantly, a substantial development grant had been negotiated with the Department of Industry to cover the production engineering programme. This enabled the build of the Workstation for larger-scale manufacture, as well as a number of new developments for XIBUS.

* * *

Much of this groundwork had already been achieved by the time I was appointed Managing Director in October 1980, with Mike Bevan taking the position as Chairman.

It was an exciting time. Mike Bevan was a total truth seeker, with a persuasive passion for being able to demonstrate a 'total' solution as opposed to 'just' an intelligent Workstation. In discussion with ex-Data Logic Alan Thomas, he thought my good self was the man to *inter alia* stabilise and support the base.

And so it proceeded. Our 'PC' was full of intelligence. Engineering Director, Keith Miller, now sadly deceased, had designed and constructed 'chips' beyond wildest belief. The PC offered a multiplicity of functionality. Its rather heavy carrying case was its one disadvantage. My car creaked as I transferred it from Letchworth to our 'by-no-means' top drawer London home of 68, Oxford Street – we had but one decent room where we could invite prospective customers and demonstrate XIBUS and the Workstation. One day, as I struggled with it to the lift, I encountered a 'trouser-less' John Cleese also struggling with the lift. His even 'madder' company shared our address.

Customer acceptance grew, and they shared our excitement of being part of something new. Kenneth Baker (then Minister of State, Industry and Information Technology) lent his full support to the project and as a result XIBUS came to the attention of Prime Minister, Mrs Thatcher.

Along with some other aspiring UK Tech. companies, in February 1981, Mike Bevan and Xionics received an invitation to a reception at 10 Downing Street:

> 'The Prime Minister believes that too little attention is given to the many outstanding examples of enterprise to be found in British industry today. The reception to which you are invited is to be a celebration of that spirit of enterprise.
>
> The Prime Minister is also aware that the success of a company depends not only on the enterprise of the founder and management, but also on the enthusiasm and loyalty of its entire workforce.'

The Government Reception for Enterprise (from left to right), Kenneth Baker MP, Keith Miller of Xionics and Tony Davies of CTL

Workstation design and engineering guru Keith Miller went along to 'cross swords' with Kenneth Baker. Other luminaries attending included the Industry Secretary Sir Keith Joseph and the Secretary of State for Employment John Biffin. Further government recognition of Xionics' success came in August 1981, when the company was awarded a contract to install a XIBUS network at the Cabinet Office in Whitehall.

WHAT WAS XIBUS AND WHAT COULD GO WRONG?

For the initial trial micro-computers were linked in a local ring network and installed on senior officials' desks in Downing Street's IT unit. These were all-purpose machines acting as both text-editing and information terminals as well as being computers in their own right. Depending on the needs of the users, they could be linked to databanks elsewhere in central government and to international computerised information services. Later the trial would add voice communication to the network. Thereby, this group of cabinet advisors would be able to send and store voice messages for each other, along with their electronic mail.

It came to pass that all was not well in government financial circles. With

'There comes a time in life which has to be taken at the FLOOD' – the Bard.

indecent haste and no due notice, Sir Keith Joseph cancelled our grant. It was now down to me to keep XIBUS alive!

I visited our user base and negotiated ongoing fees. Alas, this was not going to be enough. Forever the magician, Mike had sold-ahead developments and received up-front deposits, which merely delayed the inevitable. It was soon horribly clear that we would soon not be able to pay the staff.

Mike went off to talk to Smiths Industries and a purchase agreement was struck in 1983. I elected to stand down as Managing Director.

As ever there is a footnote to this story.

If truth be told the partnership with the then Smiths Industries bore little fruit, such that the company was sold back to it's Management in December 1986. A note on the file by a Smiths executive reads – 'didn't take us long to realise that we weren't Bill Gates, and they weren't either and that they were better off with someone else!'

XIONICS: a truly British Story

* * *

Chapter VI

The Dunlop Star of Tomorrow

My ethic, from my youngest recollection, was to recognise the sad truth that I may not achieve 'world class' and that the only route to Nirvana was to participate and measure myself against others. In music this has certainly been the case and it was also true in sport. As an only child, I can't recall how many times in my back garden, throwing an angled ball against the wall, I did a 'Jimmy Cowan' and resisted the favoured England XI at Wembley long enough for the 'boys in blue' to snatch the winner. 'Ah, those were the days.'

Motor Sport took much longer. Indeed, it was not until the mid-1970s that I ventured to the Thruxton Circuit, near Andover, one Easter Monday to watch John Pead, a business colleague, pit his wits against others in the Formula Ford 1600 race. Being a competitor, he was able to provide me with a pass to get behind the scenes; pits, paddock and all that. The bug bit me. I placed an order for the weekly *Autosport* and began to follow all that was going on in the racing world, at home and away.

Back at Management Dynamics the following day, as I waited for an audience with senior management, I found myself in lively discussion with John about the weekend events. I received a tap on the shoulder. It was the MD's secretary Carol Coaker. She gave us quite a dressing down on the demands and dangers of motor sport. 'Had we had the car inspected and all the rods crack-tested before venturing on to the track?' she demanded to know. What was she talking about?

It transpired that Carol was part of the 'scene'. Her late husband Graham was the 'C' in March Motor Racing. The famous **MARCH** name had been constructed from the initials of the principals *viz* **M** (Max Mosely), **AR** (Alan Rees), **C** (Graham Coaker) and **H** (Robin Herd). Indeed, the very first March car had been built and assembled in Carol's garage in Charvil, near Reading. Carol was a 'Gal' not to be meddled with.

Not long afterwards, 'shouting' at me from the back pages of *Autosport 1975* was an advert from Page and Moy, the then Leicester based travel company, inviting me to board a Boeing 747 for a long weekend at the Monaco Grand Prix. Nina didn't need any persuading, so we signed up for what promised to be a trip of a lifetime.

We were at the 'track' from the moment we boarded. Over the aircraft PA came the voice of 'guru' commentator Murray Walker. And, down the aisle came, none other than, 'headline' F1 driver James Hunt, accompanied by his then 'partner', happy to answer 'inane' passenger questions. What a start!

Our hotel was along Avenue Princesse Grace to the east of the Portier – down from Casino Square and the 'twisty bits' and at the sharp right-hander into the tunnel. I was up promptly for an early morning start to F3 qualification. Final qualification comprised two heats of 21 cars, with 21 to qualify. I grabbed my 'plastic' stop-watch, dashed along and settled myself close to a groaning trolley of warm French bread, ham and cheese.

The onlookers at this hour were only those who 'knew' their stuff. The F3 contest was full of drivers aspiring to F1. It would be by far the most exciting contest of the weekend and in Tony Brise, the UK had an emerging star. The first heat passed without incident. Then came Tony's turn in Heat 2. He had set a good time in time trials and was well to the fore. Alas, when the field reached Portier he was well down and the car was spluttering and falling back. He had to pit and by the time the field passed again he was last by some distance, though his car sounded back on song.

It took a couple of laps for him to catch the back of the field. Now, he had to reach at least 10th place to qualify for the final. He gained position

Nina at the Monaco Grand Prix 1975

with each lap, until, with just two laps to go, he passed by in 10th. He had qualified for the final, albeit at the back of the field. Our select band of onlookers applauded as if he had won. The F3 final would be something to savour.

* * *

I returned to the hotel to find that Nina had been royally served at breakfast by the Hotel. It was time to meet up with Carol who had flown out on 747 #2. We found ourselves at the Hermitage Hotel, need I say more? Carol was calling upon a 'new' friend. He was a man in the 'City' – the sort of guy, we reflected on our first meeting, that ladies inevitably fall for.

While we waited in reception, in came a dashing Jackie Stewart. Before I could caution her, up jumped Carol to greet him. He had often driven for March but alas he could not remember Carol. Later that day, when Carol ventured to the March yacht in the harbour to meet her old 'friend' Debbie Rees, she was again rejected. She recognised that perhaps, she was of 'the old school' and that the world had moved on.

Later we all walked around to gain a vantage point to see the F3 final. Something must have happened beyond our view, so that when the leader came into sight, he was some distance ahead of second. But, to our delight, Tony Brise, starting from last, was now on the move. Pass after pass he made through the field until he had reached *second* place. This superb drive was recognised by the local '*Nice Matin*' paper as a heroic drive by 'Le Jeune Anglais'.

***

We had a proper seat for the F1. It was a dismal day and a dismal result for the UK – Lauda and Ferrari.

Meanwhile, Carol's *beau* had been in action and Nina and I had been invited to a party/dinner at the Hotel de Ville in Menton, hosted by the younger family members of the McAlpine civil engineering company. It goes without saying that we were not at the 'top table', but being a naïve youngster, I had assumed that we were being entertained. Whilst the 'top table' and others sampled the 'best of the best', Nina and I selected the most modest of fare and drink. Imagine my chagrin when the bill was divided equally among the attendance. These were the days before automatic card payments. I had just enough cash. Here end'th the first lesson!

There is a tragic footnote to this story: that year's Formula 3 success at Monaco earned Tony a seat in the team that Graham Hill formed after his retirement. Sadly, on the 29th November 1975, Graham Hill and the team, including driver Tony Brise, were lost in an air crash returning from testing their new car in France.

***

As the year wore on, John Pead returned a few good results in his Formula Ford 1600. This class was, and still is, very popular in producing drivers aspiring to

John Pead clinches the sale of the Hawke DL2B

F3. However, this was considered a rather large and expensive leap. Enter therefore, an interim class, Formula Ford 2000.

John expressed a wish to go there, but what could he do with his current car?

Enter my moment of madness. What if I hired the Goodwood racetrack for a test session with the 1600? If I could deliver a reasonable time, I would buy it. After some instruction I set off. I didn't break any records but at least I arrived back in one piece and hadn't destroyed the engine or gears. The deal was consummated and I became the proud owner of a Hawke DL2B Formula Ford 1600, plus a trailer.

The Goodwood track itself is nice and open and the surrounds beautifully picturesque. 'Just the place for a week's family holiday,' I thought! When I telephoned ahead to the track and enquired about more bookings, they suggested that I should 'just come down'. They promised to fit me in and said that I could park the car at the track. If someone 'heavy' arrived to test I could work around that. A local inn, well used to crack-pots like me arriving to test their dream, would put me and the family up for the week. Everything was in place.

All went well. Then, one morning, along came twice-World Champion John Surtees to test his newly designed and built Formula 1 racer. Needless to say, I stepped aside; it would have been far too dangerous for us to be on the track at the same time. John however, and his engineer, were generous enough to let me stand by and watch the spectacle unfold at first hand. 'Wow!' There was more to come. After lunch, along came his new-found 'hard charger', a certain young John Watson. Surtees had been spectacular enough, but Watson took it to a new level!

***

Motor racing is well governed and operates under strict rules. To race you must first obtain a 'Novice' Racing Licence, together with a signed Medical Card. 'Novice' entrants to a race must display a Black X on the back of the car to indicate that they are just starting out. In the UK, the governing associations, the BARC (British Automobile Racing Club) and the BRSCC (British Racing and Sports Car Club), each publish lists for the races to be held at the various tracks. Drivers have to formally register an entry and pay an entrance fee. In return, they receive a printed programme and a number to stick on the car.

Drivers have to arrive at the track in time for an official safety check. I was especially glad of that scrutiny on one occasion when the check revealed that having tightened a bolt, I had inadvertently caused two rods to clash together. Had I taken the car out like that something would have surely broken.

Apart from the obvious objective of a race, there is good reason to complete a race safely and within 'a reasonable distance of the winner' (whatever that means?). To achieve this means that you can go to race administration and have your Novice licence signed. After six such signatures, one gets a 'National' Racing Driver licence. I may summarise my racing outcome by declaring that I am the proud owner of a 'National' licence (since expired).

The sponsorship powers that season had created the 'Dunlop Star of Tomorrow Championship' at various circuits for we 'hard tryers'. Although I was towards the back of the grid on my first outing, at Mallory Park in Leicestershire, I felt that with my 'active' brain I should be able to jump to a few places ahead of me. How wrong was I to be! The lights go out and all go forward at the instant. Instinctively, I let the clutch out and the *car* carried *me* forward, not the other way round!

As a family, we toured the country with further outings at Snetterton, Llandow and Oulton Park. I had an 'off' at Snetterton but recovered. At Oulton Park I was in a National Championship race. I am proud to admit that I was lapped by two racers who were later to attain F1, *viz* Derek Daly and Derek Warwick.

* * *

In between times, we found time to visit the USA. Our close Swedish friends and former neighbours in Osterley, Bodil and Eddie Lund, had moved to Elkhart, Indiana and we planned to base our trip around a visit to them. I made the arrangements only to find that Eddie had to be in Europe at that time! We switched our plans and instead started our holiday at Long Beach, California. Our flight was not without incident; after taxiing for take-off, our TWA 747 managed to drop its front wheel off the concrete strip to sink into the Heathrow mud. We set off a day late!

Not aware of our delay, we were greeted at our Holiday Inn with the news that it was fully booked. Fortunately, the receptionist took pity upon our two extremely tired young daughters and managed to find a room. We threw down our bags and made our way to the top floor for much needed sustenance. Seeing our little ones, the *Maître D* enquired whether we had our 'Hungry Money'.

'What's that?' I asked.

'Go downstairs and get your tickets,' he replied, 'and the girls will eat for free.'

I was down in a flash. As I waited for the lift to take me back up, the door opened and who should emerge but Ferrari driver Nikki Lauda. I took one look at him. He smiled graciously. It was not long after his fiery accident. When I returned to the family, I changed my order from steak to fish!

* * *

For a few days, our visit to Long Beach and Los Angeles was 'all' Disney and Queen Mary. However, one benefit of our changed timetable was that it would allow me to go to the West Coast Grand Prix. Once granted leave of absence by the family, I was there in a flash and I soon felt at home seated in the crowd. When I told them that I had raced in the UK, I was showered with questions. It was their dream to visit Britain one day.

* * *

Remembering my jazz roots, we went in search of the famous 'Lighthouse Jazz Club' at Hermosa Beach, where all the West Coast boys like Conte Candoli, Shorty Rogers, Gerry Mulligan and Shelley Manne had played and recorded in the 1950s and 60s. I had once seen a black and white TV episode of the *Saint* some years back and this depicted the club in a *real* Lighthouse. 'What a disappointment' – here it was, just a large bar 'shack' and hall by the beach. I noted that Maynard Ferguson was to appear that very night, but with the young ones to think about, we had to give that a miss. 'Where is *the* Lighthouse?' I enquired of a lady at the bar. She pointed me to a headland round the coast. Sure enough, there it was. We took the obligatory photograph and retired to our hotel.

Our monster trip then took us up the coast to Monterey, thence to San Francisco, through the Yosemite National Park, down the valley and up to Las Vegas. Las Vegas was in its early days, but we organised a baby-sitter at our hotel and set out for our $100 night out of three shows. First, Buddy Greco, hot on jazz piano; then to a vaudeville cabaret and finally the star of the evening, Neil Sedaka.

We moved on to the Grand Canyon and eventually down to Phoenix, Arizona. There Nina and our two daughters sought a break which allowed me to visit the Phoenix Oval where I saw some early NASCAR. 'How could they all navigate the extremely tight track?' I wondered.

We were now scheduled to catch up with Bodil and Eddie at Elkhart. This meant flying out of Phoenix to Chicago and then hiring a car. We passed the 'shell' of the once mighty steel town, Gary. What a sight! When we were delayed by a puncture on the highway, we didn't realise that we had passed through a time zone! As a result, unbeknown to us, our meeting arrangements were thrown asunder and Bodil and Eddie were nowhere to be seen when we eventually arrived at the designated car park to meet them. There was nobody there except a large black police car, sniffing around, which made me more than a little uneasy. At last, Eddie saved the day. He had sussed that I had 'dropped one' on the times and we were saved!

***

Eddie was a senior manager in the pharmaceutical company, Miles Laboratories and was in final training prior to taking up a position in Europe. He had to go to work, the ladies had much talking to do, so what should I do?

Well, here I was at the US Headquarters of the **SELMER** Music Instrument company of Paris, France. I picked up the Yellow Pages and found their address. I rang the bell and was met by a delightful lady of a certain age. I announced myself as a musical player and that I played all their instruments. She was most welcoming and said that, if I could give her half-an-hour, she would set up a tour of the floor for me. 'It's a great pity that you didn't call yesterday,' she declared. 'The famous clarinet player *Benny Goodman* was here.' I hastened to respond, that perhaps I wasn't in that league!

She was as good as her word. I was amazed to see that every stage of the manufacturing process was done by hand. The ladies turning the wood for the clarinets did so by eye. I met the top instrument tester who himself blew the horn and, if satisfied, added the engraving himself. I had read in the brochures that the top instruments were hand engraved but I never expected for it to be done so literally.

I concluded that the Japanese production engineering would soon take over the day; so, it has proved.

***

On return to the UK, it was time to do some work, but I still visited the tracks whenever I could. Test days at the Brands Hatch club circuit had me 'looking behind' most of the time. Those who know the circuit will recognise how tight it is.

Everyone was allowed on the track on test days. This included some of the 'big boys' checking out their monster Formula 5000s. Having dived 'off the board' at Paddock Hill Bend I charged up the hill and looking in my mirrors could see a F5000 closing rapidly. 'I'd better get round the Druids hairpin smartish!' I thought. I overdid it, however, spun towards the barrier and staggered to a stop. Looking back up the track I saw that the F5000 had also come to a standstill. The driver was leaning out and laconically waving at me to **REMOVE** myself!

I caused a minor sensation at the office one day when 'Goodwood' telephoned. I had booked the track for the next day, but Lotus cars had just hired the American racer Mario Andretti and wished to give him a test outing. I was in the way. Needless to say, a ripple went round the office when I agreed to make way for the great Mario!

At the end of the season, the Formula Ford Festival is held at Brands Hatch on the Grand Prix Circuit. Everyone is there including quite a few 'hard chargers' from overseas. It's really *the* Champion of Championships; a busy day and one that counts for those aspiring to move up the ladder!

I had an enthusiastic friend with me, who helped to get the car ready, but we were having trouble and the car would not always start! We checked everything thoroughly, including the battery and I eventually made the grid. The starting lights went out – nothing! I ducked down, as those behind me rushed past. The marshals ran across to me and began pushing. They waved frantically as I gathered pace and at last, I let out the clutch and was off.

Back in the paddock, my friend and I tried to locate the problem. Unbeknown to me, pressure from my body squeezed a cable that ran under my seat to link the battery to the starter motor.

What's more, to our horror, we found a break in the cable insulation; it had shorted on the petrol tank when I pressed the GO button. **WOW!**

The day I sold the car

Sad to say, that was the end of my day at the races.

* * *

For a number of years Nina and I promised each other that we would take in a Grand Prix as part of a holiday break. Those were the days when you could purchase a Rover ticket for the practice days and be free to wander around the circuit stopping at the various vantage spots as the cars rushed by.

What a delight that was! Of course, we would carefully select a seat for race day. Over the years we enjoyed the spectacle at Barcelona, Monaco, Pau (F3), SPA, Estoril not forgetting the hullabaloo at Monza. Alas, those days have gone. The price of a seat and its attendant restriction makes it no longer worthwhile.

Nevertheless, in 1993 we made an exception for the USA Indy 500. Why? Nigel Mansell was the hero of the hour. He had already attained the F1 World Championship, including the spectacular overtaking of his team-mate Nelson Piquet at Stowe in the Silverstone Grand Prix – something worth the price of a SKY subscription alone.

Not even a back injury, sustained at the Phoenix Oval Indy Car Circuit, could hold him back as he took to the grid of the Indy 500. We took our seats at the last corner before the entrance to the pits. Off they went. It's a long race, and lap after lap progresses with not a lot of action. The excitement began to mount up in the second half. Mansell edged forward and the race became a three-way challenge between himself, Emerson Fittipaldi and Arie Luyendyk.

With no more than 15 laps to go, Mansell went for it and took the lead. Alas, Lyn St James, the one woman in the race, signalled a breakdown. She trundled round the last corner, all but entering the pit lane and pulled up. By this time Mansell was at full bore. The 'Yellow Flag' went up and the race was suddenly reduced to walking pace. Mansell found himself consigned to 3rd place when he missed out on the restart. 'What an injustice!' But, as they say, 'that's racing'.

The GP Grid assembled at Barcelona, May 1995

GET READY ...

GO ... !!

Even though motor sport has slipped down our 'must do' list, I still keep half an eye on what's happening when thinking about a holiday. In 1995, seeking the delights of Tuscany and Florence, I happened upon the Mugello circuit close to Scarperia e San Piero. I had mostly associated this with two wheels and MotoGP, but I noticed that the 'monster saloon' DTM set (mostly German, Mercedes, Audi etc.) were due to race there. Bernd Schneider was 'King of the Mercedes Castle' that year but a young Scot, Dario Franchitti, was showing up as a fast #2.

One fair morning we set course for the track. Locating Scarperia, we popped into a deli for some lunch bites, not forgetting the luscious green grapes. We sat in a park and were delighted to hear the sound in the distance of a F1 testing. It turned out to be Johnny Herbert, but what was he doing there, so far from home? Fortified by our delicious lunch, we followed the sounds and signs to the track. The gate was open, so we popped in and parked.

Looking around, it was not long before a young lady appeared and enquired as to our purpose. 'We're looking for tickets for the weekend?' we asked. We were not to be disappointed. 'Follow me,' she indicated and led us into the centre of all the action. We were shown around the control set-up and enjoyed vista views of the track. Tickets were no problem and she gave us all the information we needed for race day. 'It will be busy!' she warned.

We set off early the next morning and managed to find a spot where we could lie down with a good view of the main straight. Even the inevitable 'fast food' service was to hand, but with a subtle Italian twist which caused us to go back for 'seconds'! All in all, a great feel all around.

The racing was in two parts and intensely competitive. In the first, Mercedes just had the edge with Schneider 1st and Franchitti 3rd. Then, quite the reverse in the second, with Franchitti 1st and Schneider 3rd. The result made **this** Scotsman very happy and was worth all the hassle to get there.

***

It's now well accepted that the Monaco Grand Prix is not worth all the money, and the crowds! The place itself is appropriately described as a 'Sunny Spot for Shady People'. The race often results in a two-hour procession of 'follow the leader'. What's a man to do?

The answer: every other year, a few weeks before the Grand Prix, they hold an Historic Race gathering. This has the twin benefit of checking out the track for safety before the main event and offering the true enthusiast a dip into the past. A miscellany of race craft is on show, from the most historical to the almost up to date F1 machinery. Also, a serious F3 race is added to the calendar to spice things up, which is not to say that the racing classes do not provide close and exciting fare. The whole thing is a treat at acceptable entrance prices. It's well worth going a couple of days ahead of the race days to sample the delightful beach bar/restaurants and the jazz sounds. A 'before you leave' drink and snack in the Hotel de Paris on Casino Square should also be budgeted for.

But what do you do for the other year, I hear you ask? Today's answer is the fast-emerging battery powered Formula E brigade. This takes a bit of getting used to, for all you hear, when the cars pass by, is a swoosh/woosh and the occasional squealing of tyres. However, all the manufacturers are pouring their development monies into its development; 'It saves the Planet you know!' 'Mercedes Toto' has even got his lovely Scottish wife 'Susie' running a team between baby feeds.

The first time I saw the cars, they only ran around half the Monaco circuit and had to be changed as they were apt to run out of battery power. Things have moved on at a pace and continue to do so. '2020' would have seen a transformation. Alas COVID-19 put paid to that. Looking ahead, if you can get used to the idea of no noise, a visit to see Formula E is to be recommended before the price goes up!

* * *

Chapter VII

Data Logic Phase 2 – and 'Sale of the Century'

'Never return whence you came' is, of course, the unwritten rule in career progression.

However, being a simple soul and more than a trifle exhausted from foraging for the finances to pay the monthly wages at Xionics, did I wish to seek further pastures new? '**NO**.'

When I did return to Data Logic in 1984 – '**what did I find?**'.

It had grown in the intervening years and in many ways had taken-on the mantle of being a part of a 'Big Company'. Although the top technical guys still plied their expertise, all the old shareholders had gone. Peter McKee, a top-qualified and experienced company business accountant from Raytheon, had been appointed Managing Director.

Firstly, the Good News!

Being an 'overtly senior person', I was offered Associate Director status. I entered as Professional Services Sales but then found a home in Major Accounts Defence.

The company had built a base of expertise providing programing support for the open UNIX multi-computer system, something I was immediately able to trade across the Atlantic to Raytheon. With the pound/dollar rate at around $1.40 and different salary levels, it made financial sense to pay visits to Boston and supply UK staff.

Everyone, especially the staff, welcomed this trade. My only bad experience was when visiting and searching out an evening jazz session with some of the guys. We found ourselves in the midst of a Boston Irish pub and looking towards the stage, saw it draped in Irish flags and banners – 'Down with the English!' My Scots accent saved us that evening and I urged the guys to drink up and we were off.

***

The highlight of my second stint with Data Logic was undoubtedly the **CHOTS** programme. I had been familiar with systems house led turnkey projects (a type of project constructed so that it can be sold to any buyer as a completed product) but **CHOTS** was in an entirely different league.

CHOTS, stood for **C**orporate **H**eadquarters **O**ffice **T**echnology **S**ystem. It was a major initiative on the part of the Ministry of Defence (MOD) to streamline and increase the efficiency of its communications by developing and installing an automated high-security office system throughout its UK operations. At the end of the project, a total of 24,000 people would have access to 12,000 terminals, which would in turn have access to full secure office facilities.

The MOD had specified a hardware architecture and independent software solution based upon the then latest UNIX operating system. Moreover, the solution had to be capable of being installed upon the 'kit' of at least two hardware suppliers.

PARTNERSHIP
People meeting the challenge

Developing a sophisticated battlefield information system to aid planning and decision making in the turmoil of battle

Raytheon

The prime contractor for the Patriot, Hawk, Sparrow and NATO Seasparrow systems and a major supplier of tactical air defence missile systems

TOPIX
TRUSTED OFFICE PARTNERSHIP

A consortium of five significant international organisations formed specifically to propose a solution for the MoD CHOTS project

Cossor
A **Raytheon** Company

Responsible for the fitting of avionic equipment to all RAF Strike aircraft and renowned for its Queen's Award winning work on Monopulse radar systems

The 'Golden Rule' for any bidder was always to keep uppermost in the mind that the UK public sector procurement rules mandated that the lowest price 'compliant' solution won the day. This was not only an irritating frustration for guys who wanted to present their 'best' recommended solution, but also led to frustration for the purchaser user who had, more often than not, to suffer the operation of a very utilitarian system.

The real secret of success on the part of a 'savvy' sales team in negotiating these complex multi-partner procurements, was to 'second guess' the purchaser's assessment schedule. For instance, what was *most* important to the purchaser's team and how could that be maximised in the solution, while at the same time exercising price control and staying *in* business. That was the key skill vested in the supplier Programme Manager: *enter stage right*, ICL Programme Manager, Harry Lloyd.

One of the 'old' school and a former army artillery commander, Harry, ably supported by his Systems Delivery Manager, Roger Ashbrooke, believed in team building because we were 'fighting a war'. His first step was to 'inspect' his 'troops': an amalgam of ICL, Hewlett-Packard, BICC (British Insulated Callender's Cables) networking cabling systems, Coopers and Lybrand installation implementation controllers and bringing up the tail, me in Data Logic, the software solution design authority.

Having identified British Telecom (BT) as the 'enemy' – they were arguably the market leaders and represented our toughest competition – Harry gathered together all the consortium partners. 'At the bid level,' he proclaimed, 'Systems Integration through intercompany trust in the partnership is the key to success. It's all about communication – now, what can each partner offer?' The TOPIX consortium was born.

This is where I came in! It is all well and good proving solutions at a technical level but the real question is how to win over the 'purse people' and create confidence within government circles, for all too often formal purchasing procedures could get in the way of confidence building.

Over the years, our sister company in Raytheon Europe, Cossor Electronics, held a hospitality tent at the grounds of the Wimbledon Lawn Tennis Club during the All England Lawn Tennis Championships. Earlier in 1988, I had persuaded Raytheon Europe President Alan Thomas, that a young UK tennis player, Ms Teresa Caitlin, was emerging as an exciting prospect on the circuit

Teresa Caitlin's support team flanked by Wimbledon 'Queen Bee' Jean Fife (to her right) and my own Jennifer Philip (to her left)

and was worthy of our sponsorship. Coincidentally, Raytheon USA President, Tom Phillips, a keen follower of tennis, was set to visit from the States.

A plan began to take shape in my mind. Why not entertain Tom for a day at Wimbledon and arrange for our young 'hopeful', Teresa, to present him with the latest Puma racquet that I could acquire, via my contacts in the game, from none other than Boris Becker. Surely, this would 'wow' even the most senior US President? And so, it proved. Tom was over the moon!

Sadly, Teresa lost her game that day. But later in the year, she represented the UK Ladies 21-and-under team that won the Maureen Connolly Challenge Trophy in the States. She proudly wore a Raytheon sponsorship badge (cut to the legal size of course) in the 8 – 3 whipping of the USA. A *Times* headline shouted – 'Catlin leads the way'.

She remains a leading figure in UK tennis as a coach with Cambridge Lawn Tennis Club. She won both the 50-plus singles and ladies doubles at the 2019 ITF World Seniors Championships in Portugal.

***

With respect to the importance of CHOTS, we were able to assemble the Senior Management from the Consortium companies to enjoy this hospitality at Wimbledon. The CEO of ICL and an executive from HP (Hewlett-Packard) met with myself and our Data Logic senior managers. It was all about 'team building' and letting our partners know what CHOTS was all about. They were able to judge why we were spending their money on the bid. Cossor Electronics also arranged that some senior civil servants were able to exchange views with us, though not of course the direct reps of the evaluation MOD CHOTS team; all very proper! Technical evaluation is one thing, but *building relationships* underpins confidence.

In the final analysis, this all contributed to a vital and memorable success. Our TOPIX solution did win the day.

Unfortunately, the public sector in general and the MOD (Ministry of Defence) in particular, are not sensitive to the cash flow implications on their suppliers as they proceed through their ponderous procurement process(es). MOD took many months, including extensive piloting of the solutions, to eventually declare the winner. Indeed, it was not apparent until after the declaration of the winner that our rivals BT did indeed give up before the end. The delay had some negative financial implications on Harry's commission deal as he failed to bring home the bacon within the time limit set. Also, as it turned out, I was not to see and enjoy the end myself.

***

In the interim, I had turned my attention to developing Data Logic's Defence Profile. Within my staff base I had one Alan Cort, who was leading a small team looking at the emergence of a new 'fad' – AI (Artificial Intelligence). 'How might this technique be applied to the defence market?' we wondered.

Alan and his team, having acquired some backing from the MOD, modelled a scenario for artillery attack/defence. Simplistically, the 'battle' would be represented by a conflict area upon which a Blue v Red schematic would be developed. The basis of the computer model would be the storage of the relevant digitised terrain map. Intelligence, through reconnaissance, would ascertain the attack/defence artillery resources.

The system would hold the characteristics and capability of RED artillery pieces. Mapping the deployment of/and RED capability (range etc.) the system would project the range and width of RED fire. Now BLUE, might better set up its attack/defence resources for battle. BLUE's artillery characteristics/capability (range etc.) would, of course, be held within the system. As a result, BLUE's engagement operations could best deploy a defence/attack scenario.

Had this relevance for Raytheon's 'PATRIOT' much publicised attack/defence missile system?

As soon as Raytheon USA were made aware of this development and, before you could say 'Jack Robinson', they whisked Alan and I off on a whirlwind trip. Starting at Huntsville, Alabama, we were shown round the US Space and Rocket Center as soon as we arrived. I was overawed by the size of the SATURN 5 rocket that lay in a field in its stages. I had never seen anything *so* enormous! Mind you, the early manned Russian capsules were mind blowing. How could anyone trust himself and survive in that?

Against a background of the 1st Gulf War of 1991, we commenced a round of system presentations: the US 3rd Cavalry (Artillery) at Fort Sill, south of Oklahoma City where Apache Chief, Geronimo had once been held prisoner for many years; followed by Fort Worth, Kansas, by then largely a US Army penitentiary for their 'bad guys' – no change there, for its history was full of Frank and Jesse James, the famous outlaws; and finally, to Boston and Raytheon Missiles Division HQ, Wilmington. At this time, Raytheon were offering the PATRIOT anti-aircraft missile system as a reply to the SCUD possessed by Iraq. At our final session with the Director of Missiles Systems, we were asked if we would be prepared to take the system to the Gulf for Phase 1. Of course, we said, 'YES!'

Arriving at Heathrow in the early morning on our way home, I remembered that I was due for a mid-morning meeting at our head office. Alan kindly volunteered to take the system through security so that I could run ahead.

Despite my best efforts, I was held up by a security officer anyway and asked to open my case. 'Of course,' I responded, not realising that a business card, bearing the legend, 'Raytheon Missiles Systems', would be the first thing that he would see. 'Are you a SCUD 'buster'?' he tentatively enquired? 'Yes, I suppose I am,' was my tired reply. 'GOD BLESS YOU SIR! Good Luck and happy hunting.'

The beta test AI 'Battle field' display (left) and a Raytheon Defence PATRIOT system missile in test action in the field (right).

***

I continued on my way seeking new opportunities in the rapidly expanding world of Systems Integration. At this time, Raytheon USA was a member of a consortium that had recently been selected for a $3.5bn contract to provide a new air traffic control system across the US. Hard on the heels of this development, the UK Civil Aviation Authority was seeking to upgrade (indeed reposition) the Air Traffic Control centre at West Drayton. In short, this meant the replacement of the venerable GREEN Visual Display Units (VDUs) and relocation to Swanwick near Southampton in Hampshire.

It seemed most likely that the Computer Sciences Corporation (CSC), the systems development consortium partner in the States and a major player in the UK, would, if successful, get the main integration job in the UK. I remember that IBM (Prime), along with Raytheon USA, and Cossor Electronics (Raytheon Europe) all visited West Drayton. It was thought that Cossor Electronics, then current suppliers to Air Traffic Control, might smooth a pathway for the American 'YES SIR' approach. Somehow, I succeeded in tagging along as a representative of Data Logic (Raytheon Europe) and a possible supplier of technical development contract resources.

You never knew, some high value revenues might fall our way off the 'kitchen table'!

It quickly became obvious that ATC (UK) was steeped in a tradition built around its Marconi operating system and that a similar bespoke 'hand-made' system was seen as being the most reliable and therefore preferable solution. They looked on sceptically as a rep. from SONY Electronics, a member of the Raytheon team, presented the *biggest* and *best* display system from their portfolio.

'Production engineering and build are now the keys to consistent quality and reliability,' he argued. 'We sell millions of our displays to the public across the world in our television sets, which have to work reliably, or we would now be out of business.'

The 'intelligent' VDU could also display and demonstrate numerous pages of relevant information simultaneously on the screen thru software management. What's more, in breath-taking and radical fashion, it could display and manipulate information then held by the much-vaunted wooden aircraft recognition slats, which resided on the controller's desk.

The West Drayton people were clearly anxious and not a little worried by this apparent transformation of their processes. Grasping at straws, one pointed out that the visibility aspect was not up to their spec. The presentation at that point had been in black and white. 'What colour would you like?' enquired the demonstrator. 'Well green of course,' came the terse retort.

Imagine the reaction when, with of a flick or two of a switch the display was instantly transformed to the called for **GREEN!**

You could have cut the atmosphere with a knife!

The contract for the newly created National Air Traffic Services (NATS) was finally awarded to the IBM consortium. It subsequently transpired that the system in the USA initially failed acceptance to go 'live'. This left (NATS) with a fearful dilemma, as its required solution was largely based on the American implementation. As with all major, groundbreaking system developments, success was eventually achieved, but only after many contract difficulties and much delay

The moral of this story is that some things are best left alone, a lesson reinforced with another project that did not get past first base. The German industrial giant, Siemens, joined the UK computer systems world by establishing a base at Feltham, close to Heathrow Airport. Data Logic assisted with several low value implementations before Siemens declared an interest in bidding for an integration programme for the supply of a Command-and-Control system for the Metropolitan Police. With every 'man and his dog' declaring an interest in the project, we did not get beyond a series of exploratory meetings to put together a qualification bid.

For some thirty years, the 'Met' remained at logger heads with the computer services industry. This was a good one to miss and makes South Yorkshire Police appear exceedingly small beer.

***

An inevitable downside of Data Logic becoming a much larger and more diverse organization was the departure of 'Uncle' Bill Barrow; there was no room for him after the take-over and so he did the sensible thing, cashed-in and quietly slipped away.

Hence, we saw the formal establishment of the newest 'thing in town', **Human Resources.** Not only had Peter McKee introduced a new department, but it arrived in the person of, arguably, one of *the* leading feminists of the day.

My initial encounter with this formidable lady was with regard to my pension and the disturbing news that my previous employment with the company would not be recognised. I pointed out that Data Logic's original pension was non-contributory for senior management and to ignore this benefit placed me in an even worse position than the most junior of employees. 'You need not worry,' I was purringly assured. The 'wonderful' Raytheon scheme would more than compensate me for the loss. At the time I was hard at re-establishing myself in the company, so I took the argument no further. A big mistake! To put this in context, my previous employer, Management Dynamics, had invested £1,500 with Equitable Life on my behalf. When this came to fruition at my 65th year, this represented some £96,000 of pension capital!

***

It soon became evident that business was getting tougher. Nevertheless, at one of the first senior management meetings I attended, our new Head of Human Resources adamantly declared that ''*ALL* we have is a 'sales problem'.'

'I have established and 'agreed' recruitment budgets,' she continued. 'These have been achieved by my team, and all recruits are now properly trained. Why are they not fully employed and earning fees?'

'It is clearly *ONLY* a sales problem,' she concluded. 'What a good girl I am!'

This left MD Peter McKee with a dilemma. I reflect today that a majority of our youthful politicians enter life with **NO** commercial/sales experience, except occasionally of their souls! Nevertheless, they carry on regardless with ill thought-through schemes to the frequent grief of the business community and society at large.

Our Head of HR's final move was to transfer *all* senior management secretaries into HR. They were to become 'HR' personnel, dress accordingly and report directly to Human Resources. In effect, staff were now 'owned' by HR who could over-ride management decisions on staff allocation.

With one stroke the firmly established and trusting relationships between management and their secretaries were trashed. Secretaries often understood the demands of the department so well that they could anticipate customer pressures and brief their managers accordingly. They were a crucial part of the Sales and Customer Support Team and trusted as such by customers. No more!

* * *

The Denouement: 'ICL consortium wins massive MoD order.'

'ICL's Topix consortium finally won a £250 million Ministry of Defence secure office automation contract last week, after spending four years and £24 million landing the deal. Jim Philip, Defence Director at systems house Data Logic which handles security design for Topix, said "a substantial programme was already underway to upgrade secure terminal technology during the roll-out period".'

'Computing' 17 October 1991

Unfortunately, I would not be with them! The bitter irony of the statement above didn't become apparent until a few days after its publication: I was declared redundant on 31st October 1991. I left with a sad heart. **'In Life,' as the say, 'Timing is Everything.'**

Yes, the banking bubble had burst and that led to severe cutbacks in Data Logic's then mainstream business. I was by no means the first to go, but that was a small consolation for the feeling that I was no longer part of the 'in' crowd.

Some years later, I received a call from the then office of Alan Thomas. Would I like to go back to Data Logic to see if I could rescue the remains of the business and somehow get it going again. From a company with over 900 staff at its peak, only 19 people remained. If ever there was a case of *'The Death of a Business by 1,000 Cuts'*, this was it – 'nuff' said!

There is a postscript to this story:

I recall a wildly destructive female character called Sally Smedley in the Channel Four office-based TV comedy programme 'Drop the DEAD DONKEY' from some years ago. I'm sure that I'm not alone in wondering whether there could be a connection, for in those old days we had a suave marketing and media guy who was writing for TV.

As the years pass, I perceive that CEOs too often use Human Resources as the 'spy in the camp', whereas I firmly believe that a successful business should always be built on trust among the senior management. I recognise that there is a plethora of staff legislature that has to be navigated, but Human Resources is today frequently recognised as truly *the* '*SS*' as in the darkest days of the Third Reich.

***

Chapter VIII

Stargrove Enterprises

Redundancy came as a profound shock. Nina and I had just returned home from a holiday in Portugal on 31st October 1991 with our great family friends Mike and Pauline Barker when the telephone rang. It was John Wilson, Data Logic General Manager. Quite simply, he informed me that I had been declared redundant! I know that I had lost a bid just before the holiday break but felt that to leave Data Logic so suddenly seemed impetuous to say the least.

It was one of these more modern set-ups, whereby company management immediately assume that you will turn the 'criminal' and wreak vengeance on the 'old firm'. In another example of Human Resources 'prudent' advice, I would not be allowed to even visit my office without being accompanied by an 'officer'. You can only imagine the embarrassment and discomfort this raised among the staff, let alone to me.

That said, I was treated properly. Being on a substantial Notice Period, the pay-off was generous and I even had some 'performance bonus' to claim! Being now an 'older guy', and therefore deemed unlikely to get immediate employment, I was introduced to a professional agency who would ensure that I would not 'top' myself. Modern tests were assembled and presented to me and my CV 'brushed-up'. I recall that, when at an interview by BT of all people, I was presented with a 'blind' aptitude test that I had already seen at the agency! It was difficult to disguise this fact, but it didn't seem to matter.

Of course, following the good example of Chris Tarrant's TV quiz programme 'Who Wants to be a Millionaire', it was now time to 'Phone a Friend'!

ICL were astounded at my news. They called me in and we discussed a possible contract. All I needed to do, they advised, was to form myself into a company so that I could get paid. They even introduced me to accountants, Wheawill & Sudworth, who, within a twinkling of an eye, set me up as 'Stargrove Enterprises Ltd'. This was the best name available at the time. For a modest stipend they would also handle all my statutory declarations and tax affairs.

***

Now operating as Stargrove Enterprises Ltd, I was back on the road with ICL and immediately involved with PROJECT ASSIST, initiated by the Department of Social Services. It sought to address concerns about the evident lack of control in the vast area of People Benefits! Unscrupulous claimants, it was felt, could raid the diverse benefit options then available, to the effect that money was leaking away in a veritable flood through lack of proper controls. PROJECT ASSIST was conceived to look out for and monitor multiple invalid claims. Simplistically, these occurrences would be identified by applying a National Insurance Number check across all claims and thereby weed-out invalid multiple claims and consequent invalid overpayments.

ICL, as prime contractor, was in discussion with Hoskyns, then a significant systems house in the IT industry, majoring on the improvement of techniques in the development cycle of computer system(s) design and implementation. ICL took me on the ASSIST proposal as Programme Manager and to prepare a quotation to implement the system on ICL hardware.

With ICL's Slough and Bracknell offices filled to overflowing with the normal business of the day, I found myself and my project office at Hedsor House, an executive country house not far from Cliveden House – scene of the notorious 'goings on' that led to the Profumo Affair in 1963. A chalet had been erected in the back garden and all-in-all this made a perfect environment for contemplation and solution building. I took as my main job, the construction and production of the sales proposal. Although the Government's initial Requirement Statement clearly highlighted the objectives for the system, as usual with such requirements, they masked a myriad of exception conditions. These included the interaction with the other systems that had been built in piece-meal fashion in response to ever evolving Parliamentary budgets.

Delivery Assurance

The ICL/Hoskyns consortium welcomes the responsibility for the provision of a total service for the ASSIST user.

Timely delivery of a usable ASSIST system will be achieved by incorporating into the programme:

- an optimum size development team with appropriate management. This will ensure that the development remains on track. At the same time it allows the flexibility to include refinements to the system resulting from discussions with the users.

Jim Philip

The team worked hard and a solution took shape. Long hours were spent on areas of possible exposures and we finally arrived at a costing. ICL and Hoskyns negotiated an inter-company agreement and the costed proposal was duly presented to HM Government and won the day. Off we went to Newcastle and Longbenton.

**

Ask anyone in Newcastle about Longbenton and you will receive a knowing smile. It's a veritable civilian barracks and all that conveys. One has the impression that every Newcastle family would have at least one family member employed on the vast site. It was *the* home for many 'live' government financial systems. Building and testing ASSIST against subsets of the live benefit systems was tough going. As predicted, exception conditions not uncovered at the bid stage, caused delays and ate into project budgets.

It was the same, if not worse, for other struggling programmes on site. One day I ventured into the so-called Support Office for the developing Child Support System. All I could see were sleeping bags? Against advice, the then Conservative Government representative had insisted that the system 'go-live' and the entire staff had literally been 'sleeping on the job' in order to meet the target. Exception conditions rained down upon the support team led by Arthur Andersen, as they tried to hold the system together. Once again, I had occasion to reflect on my notion that inspirational 'clever' guys, who can conceive breakthrough ideas, need to be taken aside to have their straight lines tested for population variables. As we all **now** know, the Child Support System had to be eventually cancelled. Indeed, at a later date, the then mighty Arthur Andersen, succumbed to total company annihilation when attempting the global linking of patients' records for the National Health System.

Although we were making sensible progress with ASSIST it was our turn to discover a flaw in our design which would inhibit 'live' system running. Perhaps naively, I decided to test this prophecy with the DSS programme manager. We met in what I requested to be an informal 'off the record' chat. 'How should we respond?' I enquired, feeling that it was too critical an issue to pass by.

I did not bargain on the ensuing panic. A meeting with senior ICL management would have to be convened and in due course I was summoned to an all-party meeting in Central London. Only the evening before I had been called by my mother's care home in Aberdeen to tell me that she was on the 'Way-Out' and with a request for me to be there. I decided that I *had* to attend the meeting, but I would be on the next available plane.

The phone rang for me as the meeting commenced. It was Nina with the inevitable news that my mother had passed away. I returned to the meeting only to find that the DSS manager had taken fright. He was talking to the project board and recommending that the project be cancelled. 'What is your call?' they asked?

'It looks like I have just wasted my time,' I replied curtly. 'I have just been told that my mother has died.'

The meeting winced. The parties met again and decided to cancel the project; the DSS would however, negotiate a settlement so that the suppliers at least broke even – 'talk about second prize!

* * *

Although the ASSIST project ended abruptly, I was not held wholly responsible. For a while I was sent off to Essex to look after more typical developments. I then received a telephone call from an old friend and former colleague, Duncan Moore.

Some time back Duncan, an ex-IBM'er, had joined Alan Thomas at Data Logic to head up the company's push into the financial world. It was all happening then, not only did DL have an office Word Processing product, but the 'clever boys' had devised an interactive computer system to support the 'City' Trading Room. It was a boom time for Data Logic and of course Raytheon; a time still referred to as, the 'bubble'.

Though I envied their success from my public sector eyrie in Newcastle, 'all good things do come to an end' and it did not take long for the 'bubble' to burst in spectacular fashion. Duncan saw the writing on the wall and took leave of Data Logic while I hung-in, only to be declared redundant a short while afterwards in the inevitable reorganisation of the company. But I could never have anticipated the next turn of events.

Ex-Cossor man, David Steadman, now heading up the Raytheon Ventures management team in the USA, was looking for an executive to manage Visibility Inc., a European subsidiary based in Warrington, Cheshire. Visibility had developed software to automate the management of aircraft maintenance for airlines. This had been successfully installed in both the USA and in Ireland with Aer Lingus.

Who better to head things up than the now available **Duncan Moore**? However, before he could take up the offer, the top position in the US suddenly also became vacant and was offered to him. Duncan was soon off to the States, but not before recommending my good self, **JIM PHILIP**, for the vacancy he had now created. David Steadman gave his blessing and in that round-and-about manner, I ended up as **Managing Director – Visibility Europe!**

* * *

The primary product in the portfolio was VISaer; a package developed in the US, offering airlines operational maintenance management support for their aircraft. For instance, a Boeing product would typically be delivered to an airline along with a mandatory service schedule profile, usually in the form of a bulky hardback maintenance manual. Why not transfer this to an active computer system? 'Seemed like a good idea!' At the press of a button, maintenance schedules could be produced, actions flagged and repair stock levels maintained. In short, aircraft maintenance history would be preserved.

When I arrived at my new office in Warrington, Visibility Europe in the UK seemed to be unsure as to which direction it should take, as approaches to UK based airlines had garnered no interest in VISaer. Its only major European airline customer, Aer Lingus was of course based in Ireland, and it came as no surprise that they showed a preference to deal directly with Boston. Nevertheless, they had a support facility in London at Heathrow, so I made a swift visit to Dublin to clarify allocation of responsibilities in the area of local UK support. All seemed well until lunch when I dropped the unforgiveable descriptor 'Southern Ireland!' Even the most intelligent university trained executive bridled.

* * *

A few minor engineering clients used the system in the UK and Visibility operated a bureau service running the software, thus satisfying some low volume requirements.

Enter the UK's 'top' technician, Gerry Croarkin. He had visited the laboratories in Boston and steeped himself in the VISaer software architecture and its latent capabilities. 'YES, it had been developed with the airlines in mind,' he surmised, 'But why stop there? Surely any complex engineering build requiring a post-sale maintenance manual might be a suitable candidate for the system. The product inherently provided a rules-based maintenance solution. Repair(s) stock control was part of the package.'

Gerry arrived at Warrington intent on proving his theory. 'Sales Manager,' he commanded. 'Go out and find me a major account prospect.'

I look on as Gerry Croarkin explains the VISaer Project to HRH Prince Michael of Kent

And find a prospect he did – FKI Engineering – a then major manufacturing and engineering concern in the UK. In my systems house days, a chargeable consultancy study would have been sold, but Visibility was product based, wasn't it? FKI possessed a forward-thinking MD. Gerry started work.

I found an untidy situation when I arrived at Warrington. Gerry was already well-down the road of proving his theory, but instead of forming a team with the Sales Manager, he had side-lined him completely, so-much-so that 'Mr Sales' wanted to leave. Indeed, Gerry was so territorial about his findings that he was on the point of offering his services directly to FKI, thus bypassing Visibility altogether. Of course, this unsettled the MD of FKI. I reflected that, 'It's OK persuading an MD, but he has got to sell the concept to his Board.' At that time, the technical report ran to many pages – 'Not the 'dainty dish' to put before a King!'

I concluded that a costed management summary was needed. Gerry reluctantly outlined the key solution elements and I extracted the benefits to the customer and prepared a cost estimate. The proverbial report of 'not more than 10 pages' was thus presented to the Directors' meeting by the MD, myself and the sales manager. Gerry sat in attendance at the back of the room. We won the day!

The announcement that a major account had been won in the UK did much for Duncan in Boston and myself in Warrington. I rightly surmised that, in spite of everything that had gone before, Gerry would not be able to resist delivering the system for Visibility. As a result, we were able to project and deliver a YEAR 1 profit to the bottom line – a first for the fledgling company. Duncan being the ex-IBM man he was, entertained us all in Barbados for a short year-end celebration.

YEAR 2 progressed steadily with some minor sales, an increase in bureau activity and systems maintenance revenues. This time Duncan took us to Monterey on the American West Coast for an International User Conference. I had to present to the meeting and did not let the side down.

I hired the complete works of kilt and Scottish daywear. This was much appreciated and, as I crossed the hotel quadrangle to the conference hall, I could have had my 'pick'; if you know what I mean.

The Highland 'White Knees' of Monterey!

* * *

As the saying goes, 'all good things come to an end'. Raytheon Ventures decided to off-load the non-airline part of Visibility Inc. and Duncan had to stepdown. Raytheon had wished to keep VISaer strictly pointed at their prospect airline customers.

It was 1999, the year of the Rugby World Cup, but alas, politically, I could not invite Duncan to the Final in Cardiff's newly completed Millennium Stadium. I was able though, to sneak him to Paris for the England v South Africa quarter final. I also invited two of my ICL CHOTS battle champions, Harry Lloyd and Roger Ashbrooke. It should be noted that England were beaten by Jannie de Beer who played for London Scottish (5 drop goals)!

It was now a matter of time before the acquiring company paid Warrington a visit. We had only a small amount of airline revenue, so it was a clean break from Raytheon. I gave them all the help I could only to find that once again I was to be escorted from the site. Where was 'SS' when I needed her? As I held an accounting Qualification, I couldn't have been *just* a 'salesman'!

***

Chapter IX

Tales of the 'Funny Shaped Ball' – Country, Club

In this 'topsy turvy' high tech world how does one maintain personal contact with business colleagues as we shift from one opportunity to another? Unfortunately, and more often than not these days, such separation is thrust upon us in the form of abrupt decision making above our control.

Such was the case with my friend Duncan Moore. You will recognise him from our stints with Data Logic and most recently with Raytheon and VISaer. Duncan had decided to move to Dorset with his good lady wife, but he still retained an active interest in a manpower consultancy with his 'head-hunter' colleague from Camp Road, Gerrards Cross.

Duncan supports Welsh Rugby (someone has to) and had been an active member of the London Welsh club at Old Deer Park in Kew. I was just round the corner at the Richmond Athletic Ground supporting London Scottish and of course the 'boys in blue'. With Duncan now in Dorset how could he maintain contact with the 'funny shaped ball' game. Here was an opportunity for me to develop my sports reporting skills as I, by email, kept him informed. **Now read on ...**

***

Country

Down the years, history has documented times when the Scots came decidedly second – Flodden in 1513, Culloden in 1746, and more recently Wembley (round ball game) in 1961 – almost 10 past Haffey! Now I fear that we must add Twickenham (funny shaped ball) 2017 to the list. **Another tragedy for the Scots.**

England 66 – Scotland 21 (!!!)

The 'Last Post' 11th March 2017

I was in Cheshire on Saturday and, perhaps fearing the worst, the ladies went out dog walking leaving me to my glass and the ITV broadcast.

Where were the diffident and sluggish All Whites of recent contests? Here they were back, displaying power, strength and arrogance. It's these characteristics that cause the 'Wee' Nations to muster all the hatred of the White Jersey and to punch above their weight.

This time, however, it was Mr Jones' team that displayed this grim visage – and from the off, I felt that Eddie had transposed all the vile determination of All Black sides into his squad and this they implemented to the full. It even extended into the overtime period when, instead of the customary kick to touch, the full weight of the 'Southern Seas' pounded the Scots' line for over three minutes. This was only terminated by the chirpy Care performing a 'Chris Ashton' style swallow dive to plunge the dagger further in.

'Chirpy' Care performing a 'Chris Ashton' style swallow dive

It all started with an over-exuberant tackle by Fraser Brown on the powerful Daly – did he go over too easily I surmised? Off went the Scot and by the time he returned it was 10–0. The first scrum produced the expected penalty against the 'Blues'. Injuries mounted and in true All Black tradition Scotland's best player, Stuart Hogg, found himself on the medical table by the 17th minute. His replacement quickly followed only a few minutes later. The Scots were dismantled, shell shocked and clutching at straws. All this occurred under the surveillance of a French referee! Had he not heard of the 'Auld Alliance'? In my scanning of the press reporting it was only the unlikely source of Brian Moore who pointed to a head high Hartley tackle, a straight arm from Nathan Hughes and Itoje's disparaging ruffling of a desperate Scot's hair! Is this what they teach at Harrow these days? No sign of any yellow card!

It's at a time like this that in modern parlance we have to look for the 'positives' …? Well, we did score three well worked tries and the 'Grays', brothers Jonny and Richie, did their best to stay in the fight whilst all around had lost their heads. In the final analysis we just ran out of players.

Against both Ireland and Wales, the Glasgow contingent had kept together but the English revealed them to be just a goodish club side. At the interval, I marvelled at the calm intelligence of Johnny 'Wilko' as he observed that the Scots, having had such a bad start, had to learn to regroup and not go for broke when they were further torn apart. 'Wilko' outclassed Woodward in his analysis.

I had spent the week trying to persuade my Welsh friends not to spoil the finale of the 6 Nations Series by beating the Irish, but to no avail. Enter referee Wayne Barnes of ENGLAND! Was it not a few years ago that Mr Barnes managed to contrive an All Blacks victory over a stupendous Ireland side and from the most unlikely position on the scoreboard? This even culminated in a re-take of the final conversion kick to reverse the result. Not a sign of a 'Jack Nicklaus' moment there.

In this instance, a yellow card for Ireland's playmaker, Sexton, encouraged the rejuvenated Welsh side to snatch the lead which they were not to relinquish. Almost at the death, an inevitable Irish try was chalked off by a technicality. Wales broke out; Sexton panicked and was charged down for 'goliath' Roberts to gain the line to confirm the win.

* * *

Scotland 25 – England 13

'Revenge' – 24th February 2018 (plus the 'warm up match')

Murrayfield Victors

As it's been some ten years in the coming, I felt compelled to sit down at the keyboard.

All last week at band practices, I had been joshed by friends eager to prod my nervy disposition about the outcome of the forthcoming contest at Murrayfield. They fell into two camps: 1) the English with false good wishes, confident in the outcome; 2) all other nations who genuinely wished the Scots to raise their game to beat the arrogant 'buggers' for the good of everyone else. In truth, I felt that the All-White juggernaut would more than likely dampen and extinguish all the Scots' 'Froth'!

But there was hope. Early on Saturday morning whilst scanning the small print in the '*Torygraph*' I noted that, unbelievably, the Scotland's U20 XV had won against the English, albeit by a narrow margin. I recalled that this had seldom occurred at Age Group level. Could this be an omen for things to come?

THE FIRST COURSE

The 'warm up' act of Ireland v Wales presented much of what was best in the game of rugby today. The Irish team missing some key players, but master minded by No.10 Jonny Sexton (razor sharp pass to Stockdale – try) and the forever probing No.9 Connor Murray, attacked with great imagination and discipline. Their forwards hunted as a pack of eager wolves and it appeared that the Welsh would soon be put to the sword. However, Wales, with a confident Dan Biggar restored and Halfpenny's solid and assured kicking, contrived to counter the Irish onslaught. Biggar at last appeared to have left his 'operatics' at home and concentrated on pushing back the Irish with a calm mixture of well-judged punts and line passes. So much so that when we looked up at the scoreboard Wales were leading!

Of course, it did not last as the Irish pack led an onslaught on the line and opened up a 14-point lead through a Healy try. We all thought this was to be the beginning of the end but almost immediately Wales countered with a try from Shingler, converted by the ever-reliable Halfpenny. The Irish resumed the attack. Wales were penalised but Sexton opted to run for the corner instead of taking the points which would have seen Wales having to score twice. Sexton went off and the Irish appeared to go off the boil. Murray restored a 10-point lead with a penalty, but Wales came roaring back. Winger Evans scored and it was now down to a 3 points difference.

At the death, with the Irish stuttering and Carbery desperately trying to find his feet to control matters, Wales attacked with purpose. It would be the last play, but Wales, instead of 'going through the phases', elected to go for broke to win outright. It was not to be. A 'match winning' long pass was intercepted by the Irish flyer Stockdale and the game was lost.

Everyone agreed that the Irish had always looked the winners, but the scoring sequence had in fact nearly contradicted this. Wales might just have 'nicked it'.

THE MAIN COURSE

The Calcutta Cup contest appeared to engage even before the kick-off! The camera caught an 'off the ball' fracas involving Owen Farrell and the Scotland No.8 as the teams withdrew to the changing rooms to prepare.

Scotland kicked off and my initial take was to see the barnstorming England No.8, Nathan Hughes, put his head down and charge the Scots' line. The line broke and Hughes made some yards until the Scots regrouped and a subset managed to ground him. It is well reported how the faster Scots' forwards then managed to gain possession through a determined but controlled ferocity and, unlike last year at Twickenham, the English forwards seemed to be taken off guard. At once the English mass appeared a little fractured and uncertain.

The Scots pressed forward, and the ever-calm Laidlaw began to release a rejuvenated Russell who assumed responsibility for the attack strategy. English uncertainty spread to scrum half Care who appeared to lose cohesion with his backs. A penetrating Scots attack saw Russell poke the ball through a retreating defence for the bounce to favour centre Huw Jones (pictured below) who showed his speed, strength and skill to score.

The Scots also had a plan to counteract the lurking danger of winger Jonny May. May appeared apparently in the clear with the ball and went for it only to be pounced upon by two Scots' tacklers, with a third picking up the pieces. This danger was extinguished at source.

Scotland broke out again from the deep with Russell throwing out a long-looped pass. I gasped but here was Jones again running at full tilt though the English first line of defence. He was finally downed only for the ball to be recycled. The Scots had their 'tails' up with even hooker McInally joining in. Russell picked his moment and looped again to Maitland for him to score in the corner. A third try came with Huw Jones replaying his 'French' line break and scoring with two despairing defenders clinging to him. Half time arrived with Scotland leading 22 – 6.

How would the English respond? Only 4 minutes into the second half we had our answer – Farrell broke through cleanly, converted his try and it was 'game on'.

The Scots' forwards dug in and tightened their grip on the English forwards. Here I must make mention of referee Nigel Owens. He was decisive in his arbitration of the 'dark arts' of the forwards. He quickly dismissed English protests with clear explanations. On two occasions it appeared that the English had scored but had to acknowledge errors in the process.

The Scots survived these vital minutes and again took the game to England. Coach Jones sent on his 'finishers', one of whom was immediately sent packing for an 'armless' tackle. Russell converted a resulting penalty. The English had now to score two tries to recover the situation.

How they tried

Wave after wave of English 'beef' assaulted the Scots' line but it held firm and England lost what was left of its attack strategy. This could be summarised by the efforts in vain of Robshaw. Forever the trier he had neither the speed nor the finesse to break through.

I confess to 'pacing' the room and counting down the last 10 minutes. However, the Scots' players 'to a man' had entered the ZONE as we say in Jazz. My last impression was of Jonny Gray standing aloof having repelled another desperate onslaught and gained a turnover penalty. The day was won!

***

Club – LONDON SCOTTISH REACH FOR THE SKY

Before I continue with my 'tales of the funny shaped ball' and regale you with reports directly from the touchlines of my beloved London Scottish Rugby Football Club, allow me to tell you something about the Club's recent history and its future challenges.

Let me begin with a short character reference:

London Scottish Rugby Football Club was founded in 1878 and resides at Richmond Athletic Ground (though plans are afoot for a move to a new ground, with Esher mentioned as a possibility). It has always sought to operate within perceived financial constraints and to preserve a tradition of straight dealing, while also promoting collective and individual ambition; many of its players have progressed to greater things over the years. Successful management has seen the Club recover from the 'dark-days' of 1998/99 (more about those in a moment) to an established place in the Greene King IPA Championship league.

London Scottish reach for the sky

THE 'DARK DAYS' AND BEYOND

In 1987 the English Rugby Football Union (RFU) established a National League structure for the rugby fraternity. The game developed such that the top tier Premiership, supported by the Union, turned professional in 1996. Meanwhile, the Championship (second tier), again with some support from the RFU, strives to prosper (*nae* exist) between the professional, semi-professional and downright amateur status.

London Scottish FC responded to the new set up by establishing a legal-entity-limited-company to represent the 1st XV. Despite a promising start to the professional era with a place in the Premiership, the Club's success was short lived. At the end of the 1998/99 season, the professional side was forced into Administration. Though the Club was fortunate in retaining its original amateur status, it nevertheless suffered an effective demotion of 9 leagues in order to regain admission to the National structure.

It would be a long journey back from playing rugby at its lowest level, but in 2011, Scottish gained its place in the, now, Greene King IPA sponsored Championship. Having started the season with three straight losses, promotion looked unlikely. However, a run of 26 straight victories, following that inauspicious start, meant that the promotion battle was decided in dramatic fashion on the final day of the season: a straight fight between London Scottish and Barking. London Scottish prevailed!

After a further consolidation, Scottish secured 3rd place in the Championship in 2013/14, their highest finish in 15 years of campaigning. They narrowly missed out in the play-offs, coming fifth on the ladder. The following season again saw the team reach the 3rd spot and a place in the play-offs.

* * *

Today's Challenge – The Future of UK Rugby -2020

Without taking account the unforeseen threats of COVD-19 to the game of rugby, there were other challenges that prompted me to send this missive to the London Scottish executive early in 2020:

> 'This I fear, may be the last throw of the dice. I have been sending in this message for over 10 years now. I am motivated again as I read sports commentator Stephen Jones in this morning's *Sunday Times*. Given the crumbling state of the UK game I am resending my most recent thoughts. These are not wholly cogent, but I contend that it at best offers a vision forward for our great side.
>
> The most recent treatment of London Scottish in today's league system has caused me to review more generally what's happening in UK's club rugby with respect to the England based clubs. Arguably, the RFU has lost total control. The senior English clubs are going their own way and the existing English league system will become a poor relation of a multi-national Premiership elite.
>
> The participation of the 'historical' clubs is on the wane and with a few well-funded exceptions will never return e.g., the Orrels, Fyldes etc. Even Bedford are cosying up to the Premiership club Northampton.
>
> In this general picture, the Exile clubs only survive in sufferance through dogged persistence. London Irish defy the inevitable through their inability to accept reason and pure logic. London Welsh blew their chance through an overbearing reliance on their past reputation. Good old London Scottish just seek to be admired for their purist attitude to the history of the game.
>
> However today, the almost ignored PRO 14 League, has clearly demonstrated on the Euro Championship front that the merit of its top clubs arguably equals, indeed often exceeds, that of the Premiership. For all sorts of reasons, when it was only the PRO 12, the Exile clubs historically missed out in joining the 'outlaws' band. My own protestations some years ago were rejected on the grounds that London Scottish could not, under the

rules of the RFU, operate in a non-English league within the London area.

Is it now not time for the devolved nations to contemplate the PRO 14 as an enhanced 'Championship' league? Today I hear that they are looking elsewhere towards the Southern Hemisphere. I feel that the Exile clubs might warm to this concept. It would certainly add support to the respective rugby home unions. This elite PRO 14 would remain participants in the European Championship cup contests.

Given our devolved communities I submit that, with help from the media, the clubs could engender substantial support.'

***

WHAT A DAY AT THE 'RAG'!
LONDON SCOTTISH FC v ESHER RFC, APRIL 2012
PREAMBLE

There are some days in one's life which forever stand out and remain in the fond memory. In Rugby, I recall Edwards' try for the Barbarians against the All Blacks and the David Sole 'slow march' in 1990 when, against all odds, 'we' defeated Carling's invaders and gained the Grand Slam. Perhaps this tussle at Richmond Athletics Ground, between London Scottish and Esher in April 2012, cannot be rated at quite the same level but for a club encounter I have seldom experienced such collective endeavour, determination and commitment from two sides. This was to be a relegation battle.

BEFORE THE 'OFF'

Following on from witnessing the Esher slaughter of Plymouth Albion the previous Saturday, I had spent a week of disturbed nights fretting about the match and boring every musician I played with as to how important this all was! I am sure that they all thought that 'poor old' Jim was taking leave of his senses. On Thursday I found an excuse to pop down to Richmond on the pretext that I could pick up the match stand tickets. I had previously sent the club an unsolicited email account of my experience at Esher and I was pleased to find out that this had been read and passed on to the 'appropriate operational management'. I sensed from the office personnel that club confidence was, shall we say, not at its highest. It seemed that injuries to first choice players had reached a serious level. Nevertheless, with the tickets in my hand, off I went to *Don Fernandos* to sample the 'blood red' wine and book a family table for Saturday.

After all the rain during the week, the sun shone as we assembled for the tapas and wine. Grandson Luke wore an appropriate blue fleece with a bright red inscription which marked him out as a supporter of the 'Scottish'. On closer inspection one could see that it boldly declared 'Canterbury Rugby', but the thought was there. Son-in-law, Paul also wore something blue, and daughter Jennifer once again revealed her emerging 'Sarah Palin' traits of motherly commitment to the cause of all things sporty.

The atmosphere in the restaurant was of the best, almost at 'international' level. A table of venerable Scots' professionals engaged in friendly repartee with a large contingent of the Esher fraternity. A 'turncoat' Scot was spotted in their midst and he had to endure a barrage of well-meaning abuse. We all reflected how typical this was and quietly prayed that it would never change. Then it was off to the ground and the lively scrum for the pint in the 'plastic glass'. We splashed out and purchased a programme! Imagine my concern when I discovered only one first choice player listed in the Scots' back division. I was not as familiar with the names of the forwards, but I suspected some enforced changes there also.

THE CONTEST

Esher kicked off and immediately had the Scots on the back foot. The first test came in the first scrum where Esher pressed hard but the Scots' eight held firm and Esher were penalised for an 'invisible default'. This recurred a couple of times as Esher seemed intent on stamping their authority in the scrum contest. There was some muttering from Esher supporters seated in front of us with respect to one eyed refereeing! Esher then abandoned the scrum tactic and released their back division which set off at great pace. Demolishing some less than fully committed Scots' defence, Esher ran through us and scored easily. The kick was successful and we looked at each other fearing the worst.

Sensing the limitations of the backs, the Scots embarked upon a strategy of 8-man rugby. With 3 to 4 forwards digging in ruck and maul and 2 to 3 hanging on the side, the Scots kept possession and gradually worked up field. Normally this would have eventually bogged down but the Scots' drive was controlled and with faultless handling the Esher defence was breached on the left and a try resulted, though not converted. On the restart, the Scots replayed this strategy and this time Esher appeared totally at sixes-and-sevens resulting in a converted score for the Scots under the posts.

Could this last? Quick answer NO! Esher realised that the Scots' backs could not hold them and, bringing their big guns to bear, they ran in two converted tries. The first half ended with Esher leading 21–12, having scored three of the 4 tries required for the crucial bonus point. We feared the worst, but found ourselves in the members bar where the family enjoyed the great atmosphere. We did not rush back and decided that, with granddaughter getting a little bored, we would walk round the pitch and take the seemingly inevitable medicine. When we emerged (and I am sure that we had only missed a minute or two of the match) I looked at the scoreboard – it read 21 – 19. The Scots had apparently struck back to great effect! We stood behind the goal defended by the Scots and could only watch as wave after wave of Esher attacks were thrown back.

It could not last and eventually Esher with two Scots hanging on, reached and grounded the ball for a try. Had he got there? There was a consultation of officials who confirmed the score. Esher had got their bonus point, but the kick was missed 26 -19; the only hope for the Scots – a losing bonus point?

A last gasp. Did Esher reach down for a try?

At this point we had to acknowledge how well the game was being controlled by an unfussy referee and his match officials. Despite the intensity of the occasion, only one brief player scuffle had broken out where a Scot had been a trifle enthusiastic in the tackle resulting in some 'handbags' amongst the players. The referee quickly calmed things down, encouraged the players to take a few deep breaths, penalised the Scots and on we went.

The Scots kicked off again and managed to keep Esher in their own half for a period. Some frustration set in and Esher threw out a wild pass which was cleanly intercepted by a Scots' back who ran in close enough for the try to be converted (26 – 26). There was some celebration by the Scots but at this point your 'reporter expert' completely omitted to compute that the Scots had also scored their fourth try and had thereby obtained the most unlikely of bonus points! We were in fact now safe from relegation. As a result, we continued to sweat as Esher once again battered the line. With two minutes to go Esher got through to score but failed to convert. (31 – 26). The Scots kicked off and it was soon over.

Epilogue

At the final whistle, there was a great shaking of heads and hands and well-wishing among the fans, friends and foes alike. Esher had deserved the win but over the season it was felt that the Scots deserved the stay of execution. I reflected on some of the Scots' 'nearlies' – among these, losing in the 9th minute of overtime against Plymouth and not least the Gordon Ross last kick of the match for 'your' Welsh. Esher had done nothing in the league until assembling a team to contest the relegation play-offs.

Despondency – Esher win the game but face relegation

The Scots will have learned much from this experience.

***

FOOTNOTE – COVID19

Along with most things the pandemic struck the game of rugby. The RFU declared all levels of rugby off-limits except for the 'Elite' teams in the Premiership and Championship. With Twickenham closed to spectators, the RFU, who had already overspent on the expansion of its customer stand and hospitality facilities, found itself with limited funds to support the game. Although the Premiership got underway, the Championship has to wait until 6th March 2021 for the commencement of its 20/21 season. There would be **NO** funding available for the Championship clubs. Government support was called for, but grants were not forthcoming, only loans. London Scottish FC elected not to proceed on this basis. Although it would remain in the Championship (in name only), the 1st XV team was disbanded for the season. It remains to be seen what transpires for this once so famous club.

***

CHAPTER X

The Youth of Today – their Future Challenge(s)

Over time, Nina and I have been blessed with two beautiful and enthusiastic daughters – Jennifer Jane (Jen) and Christina Ann (Tina).

Typical of me as a dad, my young ones were given full support in following MY greatest interests! Jen majored in sport, in her case tennis with some back up in music – the clarinet. Tina, on the other hand, majored in music, in her case the piano, with some backup in sport, again tennis. Both achieved some success with their respective interests. Jen won some LTA junior tournaments and reached the giddy heights of 48 in the UK rankings. Tina achieved her piano Grade 8 and performed with some distinction in the challenges of area music festivals and indeed going on to teach younger piano candidates their 'first steps'.

The arrival of grandchildren has given us more than equal pleasure. Perhaps it's because we can hand them back at the end of the day?

The first to arrive was grandson Luke, to be followed less than two years later by granddaughter Phoebe. Jennifer, and husband Paul, had been initially living in Kingston-upon-Thames but, by the time schooling was to commence, they had moved to the east of Oxford in the hamlet of Stadhampton. Luke and Phoebe were first tutored at the Little Milton Primary where they both showed a talent for all things sporty.

Of course, grandad being a supporter of the 'blue jersey', introduced Luke to the wonders of the London Scottish rugby tradition in Richmond. Before long he was immersed in its Easter Rugby Camp. Luke was in his element.

London Scottish Easter Rugby Camp (above) ... Luke (pictured right) showing his confident handling of the 'funny' shaped ball

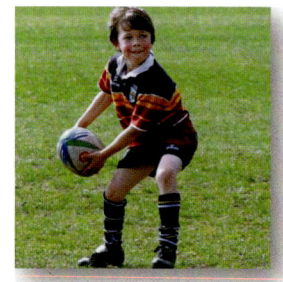

Daughter Jennifer, having not been the most diligent in her own schooling, had awoken to look out for Luke's future. He was then off to Abingdon Preparatory School where he could exploit his sporting desires and talents to the full. Autumn and winter terms saw him building his profile in the 'Funny Shaped Ball' and, in the summer, even the mysteries of 'English' cricket found him excelling. This of course trumped my Scottish ambitions for Luke but he would go on to Age Group representation for Oxfordshire in both sporting activities.

I found myself turning up to most of his contests. Aside from my primary interest in the family welfare, this gave me the opportunity to record some of the activity.

As I wrote to my good business friend Duncan Moore, 'I am taking up the challenge to keep you amused with further stories related to the 'funny shaped ball' – *I can now give you the sporting exploits of my grandchildren.*'

OXFORD V CAMBRIDGE – TWICKENHAM DECEMBER 2009

Still one of the most beguiling fixtures is the annual contest of the 'Blues' *viz* the clash between the universities of Oxford and Cambridge. It's an occasion when the hallowed turf of Twickenham is taken over by scarf wearing clans of our academic elite and that applies to the supporters also.

This was to be a festival for the entire family and saw me accompanying daughter Jennifer, her better half and grandson Luke to witness this celebration of the 'funny shaped' ball. We arrived early at the ground for the appetisers to the main event. The crowd would be entertained by a series of Age Group contests between teams representing the towns of Oxford and Cambridge.

This year the youngest participants in the contest to represent Oxford would be the ABINGDON Preparatory School's under 8s Tag Rugby team; thus, fulfilling every rugby-playing schoolboys' dream when they step on to the turf at the home of English rugby. They were to play The PERSE School from Cambridge. Grandson Luke would take his place in the Abingdon 12-man squad.

Looking down at the vast, as yet, near empty space of the vast stadium we strove to pinpoint where exactly the tag contest would take place. Needless to say, we were miles from the action. When the two teams took to the field they appeared as micro dots in one far corner of the ground, so we set off in a mad charge to get a better view.

An attentive Luke (far right) heeds the referee to calm the 'Heat of Battle, Oxford v Cambridge, Twickenham, December 2009

The game was evenly matched and full of endeavour and action. The score was 1 –1 when Luke demonstrated his eye for a break. Displaying his ball skills and swerve, he broke through to score the winning point.

Daughter Jennifer was beside herself. I turned to her and said, 'It will never get better than that.'

It was then off to the bar; as for the rest of the day, we had no idea how it went!

MARCH 2011
A LONG DAY IN READING & AND HOW DO YOU SPELL MADEJSKI? (PART 1)

My back mobility is a little restricted today because of an argument with the 'first lawn mower starting' of the season but here goes!

On Friday evening I played with the Remix Jazz Orchestra at our monthly concert in Finchampstead. It was one of those rare occasions when inspiration and technique blended perfectly and I brought the house down with my solo feature. It doesn't often happen these days which made the experience all the more pleasing. Nina was there to witness the event, but this all meant that I got to bed extremely late that night.

On Saturday we had to be up at the crack of dawn because it was the day of the **London Irish Rugby Festival** on the sports fields of the Reading University campus.

Nothing is simple. Son-in-law and grandson Luke had to set off even earlier to get to Reading University for registration while we had to go to their home in Stadhampton (near Oxford). Nina would be dropped off to look after granddaughter Phoebe for the day and I had then to take adoring daughter Jennifer to see Luke go through his paces. Finding the appropriate area within the university campus seemed impossible by Google but, a few mobile instructions later, we found the ground and managed to get a space in a pothole strewn car park.

You may well recall your own experiences of such events. Although there were mini rugby squads as far as the eye could see, we succeeded in picking out our team; the only Under 9 team (there were 16 teams in all) with kit already soiled and rolling on the grass draining their scarce energy before the kick off. Luke, now a full-time member of the Oxford Age Group squad, had evidently taken part in a school cross country the day before and appeared distinctly below par.

First up for Oxford was Maidenhead who arrived with an unbeaten record. Then came the Oxford secret weapon. Their coach is a stand-off/centre who had once represented England U21 but had never heard of rucking. However, at the kick off Oxford revealed the most subtle dummy move which left Maidenhead totally wrong footed. Oxford's 'fast guy' ran straight through the defence and scored in the first 10 seconds. Maidenhead were thereafter totally committed, rucked like tigers but could not breakdown the Oxford defence. A good start.

This strategy was repeated to the same effect in the next two group matches, won 7–0 and 5–1, but gradually Oxford's mauling style ran up against a brick wall. No one in the team seemed to have heard of getting the ball to the ground, back and distributed. Nevertheless, the group section was completed with 4 wins and a couple of bonus points. In the 4th match, although won comfortably, it was clear that Oxford's fitness was being tested.

By and large, matches were played in a good spirit and none of the injuries proved fatal. Nevertheless, I have to record that the squad, titled the Worcester Warriors, appeared to be coached by a skinhead who had his group players screaming at him in the most disconcerting manner. I can only imagine such a display of hatred being generated in a 'Celtic' dressing room prior to a meeting with England. It was unnerving for most of the spectators (certainly the sensitive Oxford contingent) and wholly inappropriate in the campus setting. It pleased the onlookers that Worcester failed to make the play-offs.

On points count back, Oxford came second to Chichester at the group stage. 4 teams were to contest play-offs and alas Oxford was drawn to play Maidenhead again. Oxford's fail-safe strategy was undone by Maidenhead winning the toss! A completely motivated Maidenhead proceeded to play some well coached and impressive rucking rugby. Oxford's defence was finally breeched and we went down 0–1. Some tears were quickly extinguished and the squad bravely faced the 3rd/4th play-off which they won on points count back. The final between Chichester and Maidenhead also ended scoreless. The guys had very little left. Chichester were declared the winners and Maidenhead flung themselves to the ground in tearful disbelief.

It seems that these days almost everyone is a winner, so it was off to the Madejski Stadium with complimentary tickets for London Irish v Exeter and the half-time prize-giving.

A LONG DAY IN READING & AND HOW DO YOU SPELL MADEJSKI? (PART 2)

I know that I am getting old, standing on the green sward from 09.30 to 13.30 had taken its toll on my already creaking back. When packing up it soon became apparent that young Luke had mislaid his gum shield! There was nothing for it but to search through everything again, initially to no avail. Eventually it was found in the armrest of one of the 'so smart' folding chairs which everyone has these days, except for yours truly of course.

We set off to the Madejski in convoy with son-in-law leading the way followed immediately by an enthusiastic mother. I took up the rear. It appeared that everyone was heading to the stadium. We had to abandon the initial routing but with the benefit of Sat. Nav. found a way in, parked in the back of beyond and hastened to the ground.

What a sight to behold as we took our seats in the stadium! Every other supporter, it seemed, was decked out in a large green droopy hat with a matching creation of an ill-fitting goblin-like outfit. 'Had we come upon the site of an Irish Brigadoon?' I wondered. Guinness was everywhere to be seen and the crowd appeared to be in great spirits, but the sort of great spirits you feared might easily take a turn for the worse.

Taking our seats, we surveyed the massive crowd of 20,000 – just to see off Exeter! The 'tannoy' blared out the customary 'music' and spectator encouragements. Son-in-law somehow got me a pint and I mustered the enthusiasm for the obligatory Mexican Wave.

When London Irish took the field, I swear that I have never seen such an athletic parade. If you were to write down the ideal physical criteria for each position it was there reproduced on the field. The only blemish was the scrum half who had lost most of his hair! Unbelievably, there were even some Declans and Kennedys on the field. The second row comprised two lampposts and full back Armitage was back from his drugs ban.

In comparison, Exeter looked normal. It warmed me to see that Exeter had one of those 'rolypoly' front row guys you can't believe could make it round the field for 10 minutes far less 80. However, he was to score the sole Exeter try only to be sent off late in the game.

The Irish set off like rockets with Armitage to the fore. They scored within a couple of minutes and generally made mincemeat of Exeter. I had never witnessed such ferocious contact and rucking, backed up by fast and accurate passing. The crowd went wild as the Irish continued to dominate. Exeter could only respond with a single penalty.

At the interval it was prize giving time for the winning mini squads. Medals were handed out on the field of play. Winners plus runners up and even third place received medals. Luke proudly displayed his prize; his experience of being soundly rucked out of possession now firmly at the back of his mind. Once again Oxford's lack of organization showed itself. Every other team paraded in a clean strip except for the Oxford boys. Still it was a great experience.

The Oxford U9 squad, with their 3rd place medals. Luke is 2nd from left in the front row.

In a thoughtful moment, I reflected on the aspirations of London Scottish to reach the higher echelons. I reckoned that we might just grow a squad but I could never envisage the introverted Scots' personality reproducing the fervour of the Irish support.

The Irish went to sleep at the start of the second half and somehow Exeter clawed it back to 18 – 17. Then the Irish took over again and ran away with it.

We left early to beat the crowd but found the car park unguarded and locked! Fortunately, there was a gap under the gate and even I managed to roll under. By the time we had recovered the cars the gates were open. We beat the crowd and returned safely to Stadhampton. Nina had been busy and we enjoyed a warming repast.

April 2013
The Oxfordshire Midi Tournament – London Welsh Sponsors a Day in the Sun!

Yes, you had better believe it, Nina and I enjoyed a full day in the Sun last Saturday – a first for this year.

The venue was Chinnor RFC. Chinnor RFC is 50 years old this year and is steadily climbing the leagues. Having been promoted last season, they were now in National League 2 (South) and comfortable in mid-table (the club has since advanced to National League 1). A club bar chat with some of the regulars revealed that a new coach had just been appointed for next season – one Craig Chalmers. Remember him proudly and often successfully wearing the No.10 for the Scotland team some years back when we seemed to manage to win a few more than we appear to today. It will be interesting to follow his progress.

Luke ready for the fray with Oxford U11s

The real reason we went along, of course, was to support the mighty Oxford U11 squad. You may recall that young Luke, having missed summer training due to cricket duties, had found himself in the 'B' squad at the beginning of the season. Also, his lack of maturing stature, together with a weakness in the tackle, was counting against him. Nevertheless, he kept turning up and the lead coach kept faith with him as he worked through the season with two active squads each with a subjective mixture of 'A' and 'B' players. This kept everyone on their toes and also placated the parent politics on the touch line!

A few London Welsh squad players have helped out during the year and improved the Oxford U11 forwards rucking (still not up to par). They also helped Luke with his struggles by persuading him into classic low tackling and avoiding full frontal body tackling where he would always come off a poor second.

Luke found himself as a utility back covering all the positions behind the scrum, excepting centre. This has restored his confidence and he has more than pulled his weight. His progress had been quietly observed by the lead coach who recognises his ball handling talent. The result, he was back in the 'A' squad at full back for the main tournament.

Nina and I arrived at the ground complete with obligatory touchline equipment. We had just missed the opening pool game and heard that Oxford and Banbury had drawn a tough match with no scoring. Everything seemed to click thereafter, and Oxford ran out comfortable winners in the remaining pool games. Here Luke played a full part scoring a touch-down and making a few others. Just like old times!

Then, like an Enid Blyton story, we all repaired to the newly acquired Oxford tent and enjoyed an enjoyable picnic lunch. Son-in-law Paul excels in this and we were soon tucking into his salad rolls and sausages, all washed down with a satisfactory Sauvignon Blanc with crisps and ginger pop for the youngsters! Does that sound like the real thing?

Oxford won Pool 1 but for the life of me I cannot remember who they beat in the semis. It must have been the wine but it's more likely old age. The final was to be contested against Banbury again. Banbury had drawn their semi against Chinnor, 1 – 1. All results, and try counts for and against, were equal, so a coin was tossed. What a way to go through but that's what the Tournament Rule Book specified!

The final started out very evenly, but Oxford pressed hard and took the lead. Banbury fought back and levelled just on half time. Now facing up the slope and with a quirky breeze to contend with Oxford broke Banbury's resistance and again got their noses in front. Now for the *pièce de resistance!*

At the kick-off, Banbury, with time at a premium, elected to kick high and hard towards a corner and the Oxford line. All eyes swivelled skywards; the ball seemed to float forever and seemingly in more than one direction at a time. Luke stood firm like Horatius. With an unerring sense of positioning and timing he safely fielded the ball and was off. Pardon my grand-parental exaggeration but just imagine the silky glide of Barry John combined with the side-step and swerve of Phil Bennett and you have it. Luke seemed to float and one by one he carved through the charging Banbury onslaught. Reaching the equivalent of the opposition 22, he transferred the ball to Oxford's pacey centre who completed the task of reaching the try line to score. Just like the Baa Baas v All Blacks (pardon again).

Banbury were by now a well beaten side and Oxford added another try before the end.

Cups and medals were presented at the Club House and we discovered that Oxford had been awarded something called the Land Rover Cup. This also meant 20 free tickets to attend the Aviva Premiership League final at Twickenham in May. The Oxford U11 squad will be paraded round the ground. The squad was ecstatic and the coach filled the cup with beer shandy which the lads gleefully passed around.

As they say, 'it doesn't get better than that' and thanks to London Welsh and Kelvin Bryon for the sponsorship support.

***

'Summer Sports'

As with everything in the summer season, the game of cricket appears to pass in a blink. It always seems to be a rain delayed start, followed by a whirlwind of weekend club and county games and an eventual prize giving. Even the most durable of followers of the game (provided you can even ascertain the precise format the contest is being played) find it an arduous spectator sport.

Who was batting first? Does that mean we have to wait more than a couple of hours to see Luke take to the crease? How often was this to be for the briefest of innings?

Luke's early promise as an all-rounder was recognised in 2011 with a place in the Oxfordshire U10 Squad and a Junior Cricket Sponsorship. The statistical summary of his first season is shown below:

Luke with his Cap and Colours

Top Run Scorers	3rd	Most Wickets	1st
Best Batting Average	2nd	Best Bowling Averages	2nd
Highest Batting	2nd	Best Bowling Strike Rates	2nd
Most Boundaries	2nd	Best Bowling Figures	1st
Highest Scores	3rd	Most Run-Outs Fielding	3rd=

The lazy, off-school, summer days find all the Age Group County squads from across the land (even one from Scotland), being assembled for week-long round-robin contests. These usually take place mostly at the sporting grounds of the larger private boarding schools which are also able to offer accommodation and sustenance. The 'powers that be' structure these mini leagues in such a way as to encourage keenly fought contests.

Of course, this is also an opportunity for mums and dads to take time off from the year's labour. Indeed, over the years, it became *de rigueur* for families to set aside one week of their holiday quotient and head for the country in support of their cricketing offspring. Luke's Oxfordshire Age Group squads were, as a result, dispersed throughout the land under the enthusiastic supervision of their respective coaches who were able to meet up and compare notes on the emerging talent on display.

Best of all, it was the chance for us as keen family supporters to see Luke in action. Through the County Age Groups we found ourselves variously at Great Malvern, Taunton and Bromsgrove. It was not all plain sailing. I can recall arriving at one such game to see a ball soaring high and mighty towards the leg-side boundary only to be snapped up by and eager fielder. Yes, you've guessed it. Luke had been caught out in the very first over!

Conversely, and to our great delight, at a local cricket club in the hills above Malvern College, we saw him carry his bat to victory over no less a county than Warwickshire! How Oxfordshire had been placed in the same mini-league as Warwickshire was a mystery, but you can imagine how the squad swept Luke off his feet in celebration. We onlookers purred contentedly. This gave us an unlikely but very welcome story to tell back home.

As Luke is now entering senior cricket, it has been pleasing to witness his progress continuing apace. Most recently (2020) at Chesham, we saw Luke open and score 83 for Oxfordshire U18s against Bucks U18s.

Luke in action, training with the Oxfordshire U 18s, summer 2020

To open the innings

Thou shalt not pass!

Take that!

A sweet cover drive

However, it's not all sport

Of course, it's not all about sporting activities. Here we were in the age of the Cognitive Ability Test (CAT) in spades. At the age of 8/9 Luke was assessed as below average for onward progress to the Abingdon Senior School. It would seem that an ability to pay for his education was not enough for Abingdon. Coming, as I do, from the North of Scotland, I had always assumed that the potential to represent a school in rugger or cricket would guarantee a place at an English Public School. How wrong could I be.

Soon after, I recall that 'the' teacher who administered the tests took her class on an outward-bound trip with tents into the hills. She found herself relying on Luke to help with the set-up. Indeed, he helped in no uncertain manner with the consoling of frailer young mortals weeping for home. His leadership skills manifested themselves to the full. Need I say more!

To cut a long story short Luke found a home in Kingham High School in north Oxfordshire. His rugby exploits diminished but he retained his County Age Group Cricket representation.

He has since passed his GCSEs and with the appropriate A Levels is now studying for a Sports Medical Degree at Exeter University. A great achievement that comes with the expectation that he will graduate with a negative balance of £40 to 50K! But what a start! The COVID-19 intake of September 2020 locked in front of computer screens and 'enjoying' all the benefits of a remote learning programme.

More of that later, affecting granddaughter Phoebe!

* * *

The Girls are Coming!

In less than two years after Luke, Jennifer gave birth to granddaughter Phoebe. Like brother Luke, she entered primary education at Little Milton, Oxfordshire. Her first sporting challenge was to learn to bowl the 'red cherry' at Luke before the family moved away from Stadhampton.

Now attending Manor Preparatory School in Abingdon, she emerged as an all-rounder – 'bowler and batter', as a member of Oxford Downs Cricket Club. Age 11 she was selected for Oxfordshire County and took part in games in Beaconsfield and Malvern on her first 'tour'. A couple of years later, in a mixed U14 game, she earned the distinction of

Phoebe in action in the nets

bowling out two of the County boys and hit a four. This so impressed Oxford University coach, Graham Charlesworth (father of Ben, who played U19 for England), that he expressed the hope that Phoebe would pursue a future in cricket. She disappointed him by announcing that her 'real' passion was for Netball!

She had already gained success at Goal Defence in the school team for The Manor Preparatory, Abingdon, which qualified for the Netball Nationals at Roedean in East Sussex and were placed 3rd in the country. As a result, Phoebe was awarded the Netball Trophy at the end of her time at the Manor. This was a huge achievement and encouraged her to continue with the game.

A new challenge presented itself at secondary school when Phoebe started rowing at Headington School, Oxford, aged 11. In short order, she found herself competing in the Blenheim Regatta. Here she rowed in a 'single' and was placed 2nd overall in her age group. We all then, as in *toute la famille* had the pleasurable experience of watching her stroking a Headington Four at a mini 'Head of the River' at Evesham. This had grandad dreaming of Henley (where the Headington Girls always feature) and searching for an appropriate school blazer!

Phoebe stroking a Headington 4, Head of the River Race, Evesham, 2013

Phoebe thoroughly enjoyed the sport, but when it started to clash with her netball commitments, it had to stop. Groan!

* * *

Her netball quickly moved from strength to strength. At Headington, her team won the Oxfordshire County tournament and qualified for Regionals. Further success followed when she moved to Didcot Girls' School, aged 13–16; the Netball team won the Oxfordshire County tournament and also qualified for the Regionals, beating her old school Headington in the final!

* * *

Phoebe's progress through club netball has shown similar commitment and success. She began with the Matrix Club, Abingdon at the age of 10. Aged only 12 she established herself now at Wing Defence in the U14 team and received the award for the Most Outstanding Player. The team qualified for the National Club Finals in Birmingham and were placed 6th in England!

She then moved to Woodley Netball Club in 2019 and qualified for the 2020 National Club Finals in Birmingham with the U16 team. Sadly, these were cancelled due to COVID-19. Once again Phoebe made her mark and was awarded Coach's Player of the Season and Players' Player of the Season.

(Left) Solid Defence! Phoebe in action for Woodley Netball Club U16s Team, 2019. (Right) Well done Phoebe! Woodley Netball Club U16s Coach's Player of the Season and Players' Player of the Season, 2020

Now, aged 16, she is playing for Weston Park Blades based in Hampshire. She trains alongside three international players and is being coached by an ex-Team Bath Head Coach and by an England Netball Coach.

Phoebe has such an appetite for the sport that in 2018 she also joined the Coventry based Wasps, so that she could compete at a regional level; their top team competes in the Vitality Netball Superleague now featured on global TV. She played in the U15 Long squad during 2018/19, was selected for the U15 NPL tournament and placed 5th in England.

Even though the 2019/20 U17 NPL Tournament[*] fell victim to COVID-19, Phoebe was awarded the trophy as the Coach's Player of the Season, presented to her by Jade Clarke, England's most capped netballer. Phoebe, by this time, had already been invited to train with the U19s and she is now a member of the team – at age 16!

* * *

You will no doubt be asking what of Phoebe's schooling in the midst of all this activity. She appears to take most of this in her diligent stride. Success in the recent GCSE turmoil saw her gaining her GCSE's: (six 9s, four 8s)! Hence, she has moved to St Helen and St Katharine (Abingdon), nearer to Oxford, for her A Levels in Biology, Mathematics, Spanish and EPQ (Extended Project Qualification). As I write, she is training with the Netball First team, though once again competitions with other schools have been curtailed by COVID-19.

You can imagine that all the 'to and fro' has placed a great strain on mum and dad, a situation recently eased by Luke's success in passing his driving test.

* * *

---

[*] The NPL Tournament was restored in April/May 2021.

Chapter XI

And then the phone rang ...

Nina could see that all the recent rushing about at Warrington might, indeed, signal the end of my business life. She speculated (correctly) that I would still need something to occupy myself and suggested that I look out my musical instruments; I hadn't played anything in anger for over two decades. 'You could at least give them a polish,' she added, 'and maybe, even look for somewhere to test them out.' But where does one begin?

We were, by then, living in Gerrard's Cross, long enough to call it GX. The *Bucks Free Press* advertised that the local Chalfont Wind Band were always on the look-out for players. Didn't I start out on the clarinet in a Wind Band all those years ago in Aberdeen? I unpacked my Selmer Series 9 clarinet. I was welcomed with open arms. Of course, I quickly found out that my wind endurance was at a premium. I needed to persevere.

The Chalfont Wind Band. I'm standing almost centre stage

In the interim, I had been contacted by my old jazz colleague Dave Holdsworth. His new Devon base afforded him lots of opportunities to play and he had also renewed his association with Mike Westbrook, who lived nearby.

Dave, who had never given up on me as a 'lost cause' to jazz, told me that Bill Lewington was closing his famous retail music store in Cambridge Circus and that 'There were offers to be had!'

It happened that I had to visit Town on business at that time so I decided to pop in to see what might be on offer. The result was a Selmer Series 2 alto saxophone in a smart mute lacquer finish ... and at a good price! They agreed to service the instrument and, although they presented it to me in a basic Yamaha case, I could not complain.

At the same time, I decided that my venerable Selmer Mark VI tenor sax was in need of restoration. A visit to local 'magician's', Dawkes Music in Maidenhead, saw my instrument restored to its full glory.

Now looking for something to swing with, I dropped by the Clayton Arms, Lane End near Booker Airfield, High Wycombe on a Thursday evening where the Berks, Bucks and Oxon Big Band (BBO) were rehearsing. Not long afterwards, the band gained an established monthly residency at the British Legion Club in Marlow, which continues today, playing mostly legacy music for various charities recalling the glory days of the big bands.

Trumpeter, Sid Busby, led the band. He was well known in times gone by for his 'Eddie Calvert' style renditions. He recognised me by name and I found myself 'depping' at a Christmas show in Beaconsfield on 2nd tenor.

At that time, the 2nd alto lady was expecting a child and I was offered the seat. I still play there to this day. The band has kept up with the times and expanded its repertoire to maintain the band members' interest and yet continues to please the 'punters' with the evergreen favourites – maybe only a couple of Glenn Millers per show. For my sins, I stand condemned forever to the 2nd alto solo on 'String of Pearls'.

The BBO Big Band: Sid Busby (left) leads saxes Rod Kirton, Mike Booker (tenors, partially obscured), Terry Bowen, me (alt) and Barry Quick (baritone).

The 'Grey Hairs' of the BBO: Mike Booker, Rod Kirton and 'Yours Truly'

The band was established in 1986 by Roy Hole. Over the years the musical direction has been undertaken by a number of musicians, including Alan Grahame, a great character whose vibes playing will be forever associated with the introduction to the BBC children's TV classic 'Take Hart', Sid Busby and ex-RAF trombonist Bill Skelton, ably supported by trombonist Hilary Spiers, who still helps with marketing/promotion and bookings. Today the baton rests in the hands of bass man Adam Linnell. The band is recognised for its work for charities and at the time of writing has generated over £400,000 for good causes.

BBO (from left to right) Jim Hamilton (guitar); Ron Long (keyboard); Adam Linnell (MD, bass); Brian Greene (drums); Simon Campbell, unidentified, Mike Turvey, Bob Hughes (trumpets);Bill Skelton, Toby Gucklehorn, Hilary Spiers, Stuart King (trombones); Prudence Sharp, Mike Booker (tenor); Rod Kirton, Me (alto); Simon Sharp (baritone).

BBO founder, Roy Hole, was awarded the BEM (British Empire Medal) by Her Royal Majesty Queen Elizabeth on behalf of the band for its tremendous fund-raising efforts.

* * *

Now being available during daytime hours, I enjoyed playing afternoon sessions with the tea-time bands 'Gentle Jazz' and 'Melodic Jazz' led respectively by Pru Sharp and John Snow. The group titles suggest the style of music they played.

But it's a funny old world! Just as I was beginning to refresh my playing vocabulary, **the telephone rang ...**

David Steadman of Raytheon fame had been called by a colleague from the UK. A major development project was in the need of some review and support in the Isle of Wight. The shareholders were anxious of the outcome. Was Jim Philip available to assume the role of Chairman? So, once again I was off. This time to the south and flying the Stargrove Enterprises' banner on the Red Jet across the water to Cowes.

In short, an entrepreneur and his team were embarked upon cabling the island to provide cable television and communication services to the population. It was a well-publicised venture across the island, but the dig was proving time consuming and expensive. My task was to keep an eye on things and work with the shareholders' accountant to assess the situation

The system was already 'live' in the Cowes section when I arrived. It boasted an impressive operations centre where incoming programming was received via large communication dishes. Most importantly, the users were pleased with the reception, which was constantly monitored for strength and quality. Regrettably, the entrepreneur Managing Director, who pursued his ambition relentlessly and had communicated this around the island, found it difficult to converse openly about the tough demands of digging and laying cable. It was my job to attempt to assess progress and validate the revenue estimates for the hoped-for increasing user population.

In order to further gain support and publicity, the MD had offered sailing trips during the annual Cowes Week Regatta to interested and influential parties. He had also committed to a sponsorship deal with the local football team. Unfortunately, he then decided to up-sticks and leave. Perhaps stupidly, I volunteered to fill the gap. This of course, meant a full-time presence at the site.

In August 2001, I arrived to soon discover that it was not just to be one normal Cowes Regatta Week. Indeed, it was to be one of the biggest celebrations of sail that Cowes would see; staged jointly by the Royal Yacht Squadron and the New York Yacht Club. This was the 150th Anniversary of the America's Cup, the world's oldest sporting trophy. The celebration had attracted more than 30 'Twelve Metres', three existing 'Js', 'Endeavour', 'Velsheda' and the newly restored 'Shamrock V'. Up to a further 40 of the greatest classic yachts had arrived from all over the yachting world. Even the actual America's Cup had been ferried from the USA to be proudly displayed in the Royal Yacht Squadron's 'Holy of Holies'.

The highlight would be a Jubilee race around the Isle of Wight following the original course of the first America's Cup challenge. Fireworks, celebration balls and educational programmes abounded. What happened in the Round the Island Race I hear you ask? Well, this time the trophy winner was the 92ft 'Stealth', owned by the Fiat and Ferrari boss Gianni Angnelli, in 4 hours 48 minutes. Of course, many different boat classes took part and prizes abounded. After all it was Jubilee Celebration time and everyone should be a winner. In the actual America's Cup class, the winner, coming 2nd overall, was 'Luna Rossa'. Where have we heard that name more recently? Our star sailor Ben Ainslie certainly has!

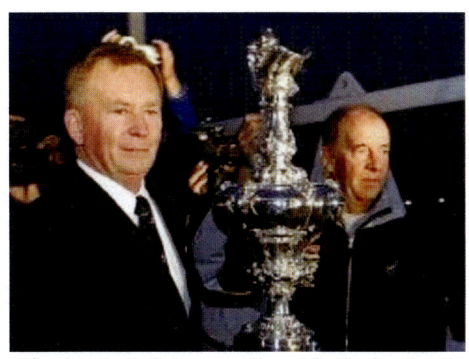

The America's Cup returns 'home' for the first time in 150 years

Needless to say, in this instance, my timing was impeccable as, in my new role, I attempted to assume the corporate responsibilities of my recently departed predecessor. I found myself presenting the island's promotion winning football team with a sponsor's cheque at a pre-season 'friendly' against Portsmouth, then a Championship Club managed by the celebrated Harry Redknapp! Also featured on the playing surface that day was his new signing, the 'lamp-post' Peter Crouch.

The 'J' Class 'Shamrock' in action on the Solent in the Jubilee Round the Island Race, August 2001

My 'tours of inspection' across the Isle and visits to the population centres of Newport and Ryde brought me closer to reality. What did I find? Answer: **SKY** dishes on the walls of most houses. Were we too late on the scene? The relentless laying of cable continued at growing cost. Would there be the expected volume of customers when we arrived, and would they be willing to pay the cost we would wish to charge?

Also, to my horror, I discovered that a commitment had been made to fund the laying of an *under-sea* cable from the mainland to Cowes in order to provide a more consistently reliable signal. A cost had been agreed, but I could not see how it could possibly be met. I discussed this with the shareholders' accountant.

* * *

One morning I was called up to the control room. 'What was all the excitement?' I wondered. 'Had something gone wrong?' The date? 11th September 2001! (now called simply 9/11). We all gathered round the big screens in the TV Control Room to gasp at the tragic events as they unfolded.

* * *

We soon found ourselves back to another reality. We had no choice but to grasp the nettle and meet with the Board shareholders in London. We learned that the shareholders had found a team from Sweden with an interest in taking forward the company and its programme. Although we would be able to hold the fort until then, this strategy was not to the liking of one of the key investor shareholders. He withdrew his finance.

By the time we returned to the Isle of Wight, the company had been declared to be in Administration. 'Horror of Horrors'! At a stroke my cheque writing ability/licence was frozen. The cruellest part of Administration is that the smallest guys take the heaviest punishment; we owed money to the boat owners who had taken our 'important' people around the bay during Cowes Week and they wouldn't get paid! That evening it seemed that everyone on the island knew of our demise.

As I parked my car in the hotel car park, I pondered on my choice of route back to my room from a fork in the pathway; take the **right** fork to the back of the hotel whereupon I could slip in and make my way to my bedroom thus avoiding the throng in the bar**, or**, take the **left,** straight ahead, to the front entrance, where there would be no way to avoid the bar. Initially I went to the **right**, but after a few yards I realised that I should 'face the music' and swapped to the **left**.

As the months had gone by, I had made the acquaintance of a number of the locals and clearly the bar was full to bursting that night. To my utter surprise and relief, I was warmly welcomed. As ever, one or two challenged me to offer an explanation for the fate of the company, but most recognised that I had been on a tough assignment. There was nothing left to do except to down a large whisky.

Not everyone took things in such good favour. The next day a hubbub erupted at the front of our company building. I was hastily called to find a gentleman aboard a large tractor. 'Was he part of the digging team?' I wondered. Perhaps not! He had thrown a large hawser around our TV signal dishes and was threatening to pull down the entire edifice, thus closing down our reception capability at a stroke.

His angst was completely understandable, but I reasoned with him that he would get into serious trouble if he carried out his threat and then have no chance of getting payment for his work. Luckily, he saw reason and withdrew.

There was not much else for me to do. I offered my resignation to make way for the Swedes.

Here end'th my business career. **SO FAR!!**

***

Chapter XII

Dawkes Music – Back to School

Back home in Gerrard's Cross, I felt that I had been caught between the proverbial 'rock and a hard place'. It's tough to live with a situation when a company you represent is placed in Administration, especially when a number of local 'friends' have suffered financial loss.

I commenced my rehabilitation with a return to the world of music and by playing various rehearsals and gigs around the locality. Looking now at my diary for that time, it's amazing to discover how active I was. Once again however, my good lady Nina sensed that this was not enough.

Visiting Dawkes Music in Maidenhead for a pack of the inevitable reeds, I picked up an advert from the desk – 'Staff Wanted'. I still had some cash in the bank, so much so, that Nina and I were off to Barbados for a well-earned break. 'What the hell,' – I filled out the form and left it with one of the sales staff.

Upon my return, what did I find, but an invitation for an interview. Even at my age of 60-plus, I had passed muster and provided I was prepared to work five days per week, including Saturdays, they would welcome me on board. In truth this was more commitment than I was prepared for, but I signed up anyway! It was March 2003.

So, there I was reporting in promptly at 9.30am to the Dawkes Shop Manager, 'young' Sam Gregory. Sam was a generous source of all knowledge. He had been brought up in his own family music business from 'knee-high'. A practising woodwind musician himself, he quickly showed me the 'ropes'. The only thing I couldn't understand was 'Why was he an Oldham Athletic football fan?' – surely a lost cause! Nevertheless, I was determined to give him my full support.

As they say, 'The first week is always the worst'. I found myself 'busking' a little on one sax sale but I clinched the deal and gained some respect from my much younger colleagues in the process.

Mid-week an older fellow popped his head over my desk. 'Glad to see some grey hair keeping everyone in order,' he declared. It was the business founder, Jack Dawkes himself!

Over the years Jack (pictured left) had plied his trade on the saxes and woodwind doubles with all the leading bands in the West End of London but then, had sensed a business opportunity in the West of London. He set up home in Uxbridge, Middlesex, just across the road from the RAF School of Music, including the well-known Squadronaires Band with Vera Lynn etc. Jack and his son Lindsay were available to repair and service the RAF's instruments. A business was born.

Now in the full flow in a spacious retail warehouse in Maidenhead, Berkshire, Dawkes Music is a mix of woodwind and brass instrument sales and associated service to everyone from the professional elite to the youngest novice. One minute, we might have a visit from Art Themen or Karen Sharp, or Simon Spillett might be out-doing Tubby Hayes, then the younger horns of Ben Castle and Simon Allen, to be quickly followed by a Grade 1 with mum and dad.

They say that it's never too late. Although I seemed to be fitting in quite well, Dawkes decided that a course with Yamaha might be of some benefit. After all, Yamaha was arguably the leading provider of woodwind and brass instruments for our customer base. It was therefore off to Yamaha HQ (UK) and a couple of days intensive training on their instrument range and care philosophy. I am now the proud holder of a Yamaha Plus brass and woodwind certificate.

One particular sales occasion stands out in my memory. A lady brought in her severely disabled young daughter. She moved with difficulty and found it difficult to even speak with any clear vocabulary. However, she had tried an alto saxophone at school and enjoyed it so much that she wanted to try one again. Mum was all for it. We took her into one of our practice rooms and fitted her with a suitable harness so that she could hold the horn. We stood back. None of us could believe the sound that she produced. It was incredible. She managed a simple tune from the tutor and her confidence grew. Literally, she made the instrument talk. Her face beamed. She had found her language!

At that time, we had Professor Anton Weinberg on board. What a guy! He had previously taught at Indiana University in the USA and at Guildhall in London. A busy session player: you name it and he probably had done it. On an otherwise quiet morning, as I processed some overnight orders, I heard him try a new clarinet which Selmer had sent in. What a sound! Calmly he leant across and showed me the new Selmer Privilege. It was the first in the country. I was so knocked out, I ordered #2!

Being a 'grey hair', I was assigned to look after the Work Experience pupils from local schools who visited at the end of each Summer Term. Of course, they were of mixed experience, but a number sought a career in the music industry. It is well known that this is a tough choice, so I always made time to sit down with each of them to review their knowledge of the industry. I challenged each with my rather demanding theory that to succeed in the industry, and get paid, they had either to be in the 'top twenty' on their chosen instrument(s) or had an 'embryo' music product idea to test. Also, they should not forget to back themselves up with a teaching qualification.

I remember one pupil had a different angle. He was interested in sound technology as a scientific and engineering vocation and demonstrated a good knowledge of some of the companies in the industry. I urged him to write to the MD of his chosen company, to declare his knowledge and interest and to offer his services in his gap year. This, I suggested, was the only way to by-pass the dreaded Human Resources in the future.

I have got to say that it was not 'all work and no play'. Being a family concern, it was full of Births, Deaths and Marriages. Alas, Dawkes' founder Jack passed away in 2006, and his son Lindsay also succumbed to a heart condition. Two of Lindsay's sons, Jon and David, took over the day-to-day running of the business. There were plenty of happier times when the young Dawkes got spliced and we were all invited. Needless to say, on these occasions the accompanying music was of the highest quality. Also, let me not forget that, before his untimely death, Lindsay and the young 'Dawkes Boys' had us up the Thames on his motor cruiser on an after-hours trip. My first time to see a pair of Kingfishers in spectacular full colour-coded action.

Wayne Bergeron, lead trumpeter with the Big Phat Band

Some top guys from over the 'pond' dropped in from time to time in support of the instrument manufacturers. Top of my memory list was the lead trumpet from the 'Big Phat Band' – Wayne Bergeron. Yamaha were 'pushing the boat out' and we were all invited to Floridita (formerly the Marquee) in March 2012 to hear him excel on his Yamaha horn. An all-star band of top UK guys had been assembled and we all enjoyed the 'blitz' after an excellent supper.

As part of its business philosophy Dawkes enjoyed close and warm relationships with the local schools' fraternity and associated music teachers. At the opening of each school year, you would see us with a van load of instruments and accessories, complete with the Dawkes' banner, driving up to various school gates to unload. They would typically encourage us to set up in a room and demonstrate our wares to a gathered throng of excited parents and their offspring. Although this might otherwise be considered pushy, schools warmed to us supporting their oft times over stretched music departments.

I can recall visiting the fabulously named Licensed Victuallers' School in Ascot (now known as LVS Ascot) to 'do' Open Day. I was on my own on this occasion. Ushered into a long room, I busied myself with the set-up. Only then did I look up to notice that I was in the Dance Studio and that its entire length comprised a mirror. I had reached my 70th year by then and as I gazed at myself, I could only see an old man looking back. In that moment, I decided that, perhaps, I should pack it in.

**

My musical ambition, at this time, was somehow to join the 'Chosen Few' Big Band, run by the irrepressible Bill Castle. Ex-army, he was one of the great characters, a task master of the old school forever lambasting his sidemen. The high standard of the band could be attributed almost exclusively to his enormous drive and energy. I already knew some of the guys in the band from my work with the BBO but there was also a sprinkle of 'top players' in the line-up. A couple of guys composed and arranged which gave the band a definite edge. It also performed at a well-supported monthly gig in Finchampstead. It is always good to tell the people and receive the plaudits.

I had rehearsed and 'depped' with the band a few times on tenor sax, but how could I get in? It's a small world. Bill had been at the Queen Elizabeth Hall in 1971 when I played with the Bobby Lamb/Ray Premru Orchestra in the one-off percussion festival featuring top drummers Kenny Clare, Buddy Rich and Louie Bellson – a memorial concert to the late drum master Frank King. As a result, Bill assumed that, as I had been in the line-up, I must be OK.

The Chosen Few, Sandown Park: (Back Row) Jim Pollard, Jonathan Lewis, Adrian Thoms, Mike Adlam, John Deemer, Me, Dave Shepherd, Bill Castle, Bill Edmunds, Brian Haddock. (Middle Row) Hazell Pollard, Alex Brown. (Front Row) Rod Kirton, Peter Phillips, James Lowe, Brian Marett, Mike Lock, Steve Waters

The band's arrangements were more than a step up from the BBO and my first rehearsal with the Chosen Few, after my 20-year break from playing demanding tenor sax, brought me up abruptly. I was well off the pace. But I refused to give in.

Not long after these forays, the then baritone player in the Chosen Few announced that his day-job in the business world had become more demanding with a recent promotion and that he was leaving the band. I grabbed the opportunity to ask Bill Castle if he might try me out on baritone. In the customary gruff manner that I eventually came to love, Bill simply said that if I had an instrument, he would let me give it a shot.

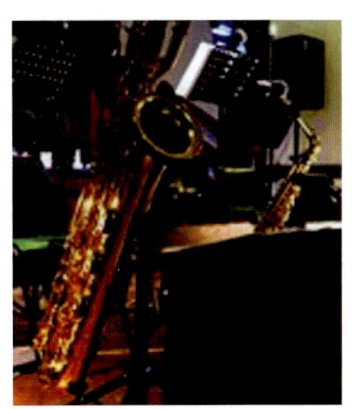

'The Beast' – the Yanagisawa Y901 baritone saxophone

It was off to manager Jon Dawkes to see what I could afford. I wasn't paid a fortune but he said he would try to get me one at 'trade'. It was the Yanagisawa salesman's year end and he grabbed at the sale to make some year-end commission. We were winning all round. A brand-new Yanagisawa Y901 arrived at my desk in a matter of days. I was off and running.

Mind you, a baritone sax is a beast. It tested my weak arms and I initially struggled to find a cane reed that I did not wreck after 40 minutes of hard blowing. I must have been doing something wrong. At last I happened upon a new-fangled plastic reed from Legere, the signature reed from Canada.

I was greatly helped in my adjustment to the instrument when I was offered the seat in the Surrey Jazz Orchestra which operates near Guildford. It was then run by reedman Mike Wilcox. Terry Bowen, an old BBO friend, who had the seat, had decided to move to the south coast. A lot of the 'pad' offered the same playing challenges as elsewhere but it's amazing how the interpretation of the 'black dots' can vary from band to band.

Sax Duel at the Surrey Jazz Orchestra: (Back Row) Delia Farrell, Bill Edmunds, Tom Beeching (trumpets); (Front Row) Me (baritone), Pete Deane (Current leader, alto), Mike Wilcox (former leader, alto), Pete Walker (tenor)

My name was spreading, such that I was offered further encouragement to be a featured soloist with Blake's Heaven Big Band (see Left), an aggregation based around Oxford. Australian Nick Blake, with his vocalist better-half Linda, had developed a pad of originals which presented a new voice to their growing audience(s). I was gathering pace and making sustained progress.

Now what next? A call from my old friend, brass man Dave Holdsworth, saw me invited back to Brighton where trombone player Tim Wade was putting together a nine-piece band to recreate the classic 'Birth of the Cool'. In the group, we had Dave in the role of Miles Davis, me as Gerry Mulligan and the prodigious Charlotte Glasson as Lee Konitz. The music itself had lain undiscovered in a warehouse in Philadelphia until 1995. Dave provided a faithful transcription. The group recorded a demo and proceeded to play in a number of jazz bars, including the late lamented JAGZ in South Ascot.

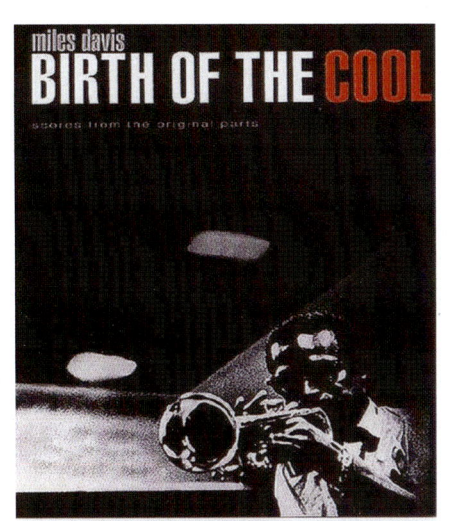

The Tim Wade Miles Davis 'Birth of the Cool' Nonet, Brighton 16th May 2006: (From left to right): Charlotte Glasson (alto), Nick McGuigan (bass), Sam Glasson (drums), Tim Wade (trombone), Dave O'Flynn (tuba), Me (baritone), Dom Nunns(French horn), Dave Holdsworth (trumpet), Tom Phelan (piano)

Back at the Chosen Few, Bill Castle also encouraged me to take the occasional solo. I happened upon a transcription of the ballad 'Song for Strayhorn' as originally featured by the master of the baritone, Gerry Mulligan. Chosen Few arranger Alex Brown wrapped the band arrangement around the solo line and I was off. Well, wait a minute. It was a 'grade eight' challenge which lasts 6min 25secs! Truthfully my initial outings were rather mixed but at least the audience liked the tune!

After some time, the Chosen Few begat the Remix Jazz Orchestra. It was not an easy transition. Bill, and his dedicated support lady, Pearl, had moved away to the country. They tired of the travelling now involved, while the constant comings-and-goings of sidemen regularly saw Bill throwing his 'toys out of the pram'. He had had enough and wrote to everyone to say that he was closing the band down.

Fortunately, bass man John Deemer was standing at '1st slip'. He caught the mood. The band wished to continue and ace trumpeter Stuart Henderson would take over as MD. A vote was taken and the band was renamed Remix.

John Deemer (centre)

Stuart Henderson

* * *

What a transformation! Under new management, Remix has gone from strength to strength. John Deemer, bass guitarist and sound engineer, undertakes all the hard work of organization and administration. His skills were honed in what used to be known as Combined Services Entertainment, now BFBS (British Forces Broadcasting Service) Live Events – an outfit that provides support for the British forces in places where no entertainment is otherwise available. In John's words, 'It's the modern equivalent of 'It Ain't 'Alf Hot Mum' – you lovely boy!' His world travel took him to Northern Ireland, the Falkland Islands, Belize, Germany, Cyprus, Bosnia and even the Outer Hebrides. Travelling up to Finchampstead from Basingstoke therefore presents no problem for John!

In Musical Director, Reading-based Stuart Henderson, the band profits from his calm and knowledgeable guidance as well as his individual talent on trumpet and flugelhorn. A military man by background, he served from 1983 – 2005 as the lead trumpet player of her Majesty's Household Division. He has played in all the State occasions for Her Majesty the Queen, and like John, has travelled the world: USA, Canada, New Zealand, many European cities and even enjoyed the mixed pleasure of playing farewell to Hong Kong. In civvy street, in addition to his professional big band work, he teaches, leads his own small bands, has played at numerous jazz festivals alongside people like Alan Barnes and featured at top jazz venues such as Ronnie's, the Jazz Café and the Spice of Life. His monthly Sunday afternoon gigs with his quartet at the tiny Retreat pub, close to Reading town centre, have acquired legendary status and regularly feature guest reedmen like Simon Spillett, Simon Allen and Vasilis Xenopoulos. He encourages band composer/arrangers Jonathan Lewis and Alex Brown to contribute their invention and skills which give the band an individual voice. Forever the subtle showman in his presentation, he skilfully programmes these 'originals' with some of the better familiar scores to bring the audience along. He demands the best of the band and encourages sometimes reticent soloist(s) to give of their best.

The Remix Jazz Orchestra, Reading Fringe Festival, 23rd July 2019: (Back Row) Adrian Thoms (guitar); Adrian Sharon (piano); Dave Lambert (drums); John Deemer (bass-guitar); Stuart Henderson, David Cunningham, James Lowe, Chris Preddy (trumpets); (Front Row) Me, Rod Kirton, Brian Marett, Simon Allen, Mike Booker, (reeds); Cliff Luke, Peter Phillips, Brian Haddock (trombones); Steve Waters (bass-trombone). Guests vocalist Fleur Stevenson is out of view

Stuart's reputation for presenting exciting group performances will always attract a large local audience response, so what could have been more natural than the Remix Jazz Orchestra headlining the Reading Fringe Festival in the summer of 2019. 'The Evolution of the Big Band: 100 Years of Big Band Music' had everything from 1920's Paul Whiteman, with Stuart on swanee whistle and John Deemer on tuba, to the modern pyrotechnics of the 'Jazz Police'. Yours truly even contributed the famous baritone riff to 'Hot Toddy', Ted Heath's great hit of the 1950s. Fleur Stevenson charmed the record-breaking crowd at The Reading Minster with her vocals and guest star tenor, Simon Allen, depping for an indisposed Jonathan Lewis, blew a storm. The promoter's, 'Jazz in Reading', made a profit and the band got paid.

Onwards and upwards!

Chapter XIII

Reflections

By the time you reach this chapter you will have gathered something of my lifestyle as I approach my 80th milestone. Quite simply, on Tuesday, Wednesday and Thursday evenings I can be found blasting away on one of my instruments in the sax line-ups of the Surrey Jazz Orchestra, Remix Jazz Orchestra and the Berks, Bucks, and Oxon (BBO) Big band. Weekly rehearsals culminate in 'open door' at month-end concerts where 'all' that has been practised is conveyed to dedicated followings of the most decerning critique. All this does wonders for my breathing exercises, especially as the baritone sax takes most of what's left of my physical energy force.

This year (2021), as you will be aware, the whole world has been turned upside down by the Virus from the Far East. Everything is at a standstill. For the performing artist, both on and off the stage, the medical profession has persuaded the Government that the great unwashed needs to be protected from my urgent sound. Sadly, it is too late at my time of life to purchase a pair of football boots, for unbelievably, the Government decrees that, at the scoring of a goal, footballer hugging and cuddling is a better example to set before the man (*nae* person) in the street.

***

Time for reflection. In recent years, with the help of my good friend John Snow I have searched through all my old tapes and broadcasts and assembled, with the aid of some tracks from previously published efforts, a couple of CDs for my own benefit to be shared with some friends and even some admirers.

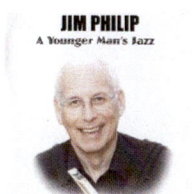

Thus, 'A Younger Man's Jazz' and 'More from the Music of Jim Philip' have seen the light of day. My aim was to preserve some of my better moments for posterity. By strange coincidence, it transpired that someone else also had this objective in mind

Almost fifty years had passed since 1970 so it came as a great surprise to me that anyone might be interested enough in our efforts from back then to reissue our jazz pathfinder vinyl, 'Atlantic Bridge,' on CD.

In 2017, I was contacted by Malcolm Dome who indicated that he had been commissioned by Esoteric Records (a label that fell under the umbrella of Cherry Red Records) to prepare a booklet for the reissue of 'Atlantic Bridge'. I sent him some historical narrative on the story behind the album.

I had no idea who was behind the venture and all my efforts to find out, including a visit to the Cherry Red Records office in Chiswick, drew a blank. I didn't hear anything further from Malcolm either and began to wonder if the whole thing was a scam. Imagine my surprise when, after a silence of over three months, Malcolm confirmed that the album had been reissued by Cherry Red. This comprised the original six tracks in remastered sound, plus two bonus tracks, 'I Can't Lie to You' and 'Hilary Dixon'. We had recorded these after the album for a maxi-single using female vocalists. The package retained the original artwork and included a comprehensive booklet by Malcolm, compiled from my contributions and those of Daryl Runswick. This care and respect extended to the marketing.

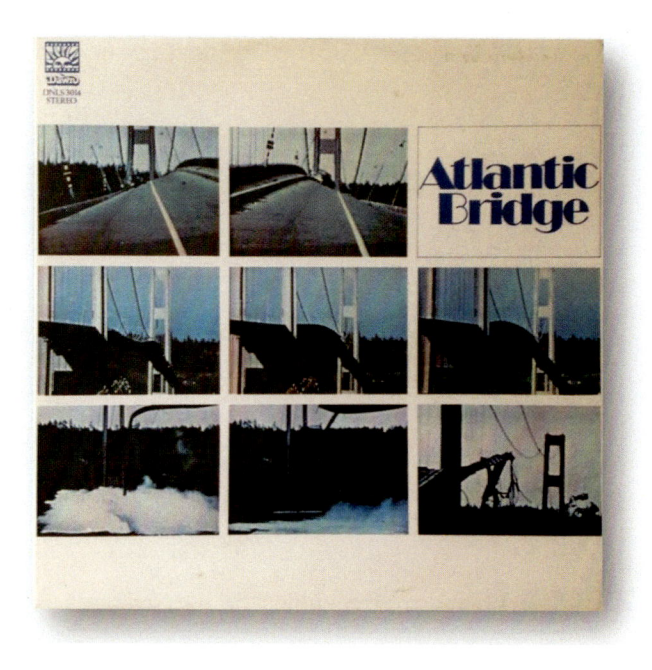

To illustrate its marketing effort, I am pleased to include the accompanying press release:

'Esoteric Recordings are pleased to announce the first ever UK CD release of a newly re-mastered edition of the 1970 self-titled jazz-rock album by Atlantic Bridge.

Born of a time when jazz musicians crossed in to the world of rock music, Atlantic Bridge was a quartet featuring Mike McNaught (piano, electric piano), Daryl Runswick (bass, bass guitar), Jim Philip (flute, soprano sax, tenor sax) & Mike Travis (drums). All four musicians were seasoned players on the London jazz circuit but sought to expand their musical horizons.

Influenced by the experimentation of Miles Davis on his album Bitches Brew and by the work of British musicians such as Keith Tippett, Atlantic Bridge, led by visionary Mike McNaught, took compositions by such artists as The Beatles and Jim Webb and crafted a highly innovative album which also revealed the talents of Daryl Runswick (a respected bass player later to play with Elton John and The Alan Parsons Project among others), Jim Philip and Mike Travis.

Originally released on Pye Records' "Progressive" imprint Dawn Records, Atlantic Bridge now commands large sums from vinyl collectors. This Esoteric Recordings edition has been newly re-mastered from the original Dawn master tapes and features two bonus tracks taken from a rare Maxi Single (also released in 1970).

The release features an illustrated booklet and an essay featuring exclusive interviews with Daryl Runswick and Jim Philip.'

* * *

From a distance of nearly five decades, I feel that most of the material as interpreted and performed continues to be fresh and valid. 'McArthur Park' enters with a blaze of sound but fades out rather at the end. 'Something' is a blast. 'Rosecrans Boulevard' points a way ahead. Although today I cannot spot this, I recall that 'Dear Prudence' suffered from an edit join and like the ending to 'MacArthur Park' is something we could have sorted out with more time in the studio. I remain firmly convinced that no other group offered a similar product.

Back in the early 1970s I was convinced that we had developed a product that could fully support the London Jazz Four (now titled Atlantic Bridge) in concert performance. As you will recall, I failed to enlist the support of the music marketing forces of the time. Also, the music critics felt that perhaps our interpretation fell between two stools of jazz and rock.

Today I am forced to reflect on my judgement. Jazz critic Roger Farbey MBE awarded the reissued album 4/5 stars in his review for *All About Jazz* in September 2017:

'Pianist Mike McNaught already had form as an evangelist of pop-inspired jazz, as witnessed on his previous group The London Jazz Four's 1967 Polydor release 'Take A New Look At The Beatles'. However, on this eponymously titled idiosyncratic marriage of jazz and pop, Atlantic Bridge has a stab at two Beatles numbers and three Jim Webb songs. There's also a final track penned by McNaught himself. Together, reedsman Jim Philip, who'd recorded with Michael Garrick and also the New Jazz Orchestra joined McNaught along with drummer Mike Travis who laid down the, often complex, beat for Gilgamesh and Hugh Hopper tracks, McNaught formed a new rockier London Jazz Four which didn't progress far. However, it did get them signed to Pye's new progressive label Dawn and a contract to record Atlantic Bridge.

The point of difference however was the employment of virtuoso bassist Daryl Runswick who was later head-hunted by John Dankworth. Runswick, one of the finest bass players to emerge from the British jazz scene at that time, was a member of the burgeoning cohort of bass luminaries appearing in the 1960s and early 70s, including Barry Guy, Dave Holland, Harry Miller, Jeff Clyne, Ron Mathewson, Chris Laurence and Jack Bruce.

So it is that a ten-minute version of 'MacArthur Park' kicks off this album with a heavy fuzzy opening sortie progressing to a more relaxed modal middle. Arranged as a four-part suite, it variously features ferocious soprano sax and multi-tracked arco bass solos plus some rather dated swooshing echoey sound effects.

The slow burning, somnolent 'Dreams (Dreams/Pax/Nepenthe)' also by Webb, originally appeared on The 5th Dimension's 1967 album The Magic Garden. 'Rosencrans Boulevard' again by Webb, featured on The 5th Dimension's debut album Up, Up and Away, has a better balance between the instruments, but Runswick is still able to insinuate a discrete but florid bass guitar solo here.

Opening in a disguised fashion, George Harrison's 'Something' alternates between brief returns to the melody and often frenetic soprano soloing from Philip and equally vibrant bass work from Runswick. The elegant arco bass intro to Lennon and McCartney's 'Dear Prudence' gives way to Philip's delicate flute and a neat 'Hey Jude'-like ascending bass run before settling into a relaxed groove with Philip now soloing on tenor sax. The final track from the original album, McNaught's elegiac 'Childhood Room (Exit Waltz)' offers Runswick more opportunity for what is effectively lead bass guitar soloing.

This reissue comes with two bonus tracks not on the original LP, both of which are McNaught originals. 'I Can't Lie to You' and 'Hilary Dixon'. The former, co-written with Barry Murray, is distinguished by uncredited female backing vocals and more lead bass, but this time, unusually, employing unfettered arco double bass. The final track features Philip on flute and is much more jazz-orientated than its pop-infused predecessor.

Rather unfairly panned at the time of its release in some quarters, Atlantic Bridge presents a frequently imaginative take on jazz rock that exactly reflected the musical zeitgeist prevalent in 1970, the year in which it was released on Dawn DNLS 3014. There's an interesting comparison to be made between this record and the equally obscure J.R.E. by the German group Jazz Rock Experience, released on Deram Nova (SDN 19) in the same year and which also merits a reissue. Incidentally, 'Childhood Room (Exit Waltz)' appeared on the 1971 Dawn compilation sampler The Dawn Take-Away Concert (Dawn DNLB 3024).'

* * *

What can I say but, '**THREE CHEERS**' for ESOTERIC ARTS who through its outlet CHERRY RED Records reissued the CD throughout its European Outlets.

If any of this inspires you to obtain a copy of the CD, you now know where to find it. Regrettably Mike McNaught is no longer with us. The world of music is a poorer place.

Perhaps I could leave you with these words from the sleeve notes of the original 'Atlantic Bridge' album as my final reflection:

Music should be a bridge between player and player, band and listeners. Between continents and life-styles and arbitrary islands of the classifiers. Who needs to know whether it's jazz or rock or plainsong? Leave it to your ears: you won't get a word out of them.

* * *

Chapter XIV

Epilogue – A Tale of Two Pianos – An Allegory of Life

My earliest recollections from the 1940s at 27, Harcourt Road, Aberdeen, included an awareness that our front room was always to be kept for 'best'. I would not normally venture to step inside. Lurking in that room was my father's quite upmarket CHALLEN upright piano (pictured left). Although not a virtuoso, dad could knock out a tune or two and voice a few of the popular ditties of the day.

Upon my reaching school age (5/6 years), our local Mile End offered out-of-hours piano tuition given by the indefatigable Miss Fraser. Dad was keen to see me take the opportunity to open my eyes and ears to the world of music. I therefore embarked upon a course. The first steps saw me learning scales and indeed the odd melody. So much so, that I was soon accompanying a more advanced student, Hazel Sangster, in an end of term parent concert. I can recall shaping the top line of 'Daisies so Bright, Lavender so Blue'.

So far so good, but one of my regular piano lessons fell on the school morning break. It was at this time that us 'wee' boys were forming ourselves into playtime football sides and here was me not getting a look-in.

I cannot remember the exact occasion, but the fateful day arrived when I forgot the 'playtime' piano lesson and joined in the game. I was later summoned by Miss Fraser and dressed down in no uncertain manner. Not content with that, she tore a sheet from my music timetable book, wrote a curt reminder and pinned it to my overcoat. I was under the pain of death not to remove it.

Upon returning home my father demanded to know the story. He was of course angry with me but, to my surprise, he was even more angry with Miss Fraser. He immediately ripped off the offending message and called upon Miss

Fraser in person. He impressed upon her that she must **NEVER** repeat such a punishment. 'I will discipline James,' he declared, 'But I can **NEVER** condone the public labelling and humiliation of my boy!'

That turned out to be the end for my first challenge in the world of music. My father decided that he needed to secure his son's education for the future, so I was then off to Robert Gordon's College in the centre of town. It was to be 'head down' to pass the eleven plus.

Around the time of my transition to senior school, my father's business had grown and, what's more, profitably. He invested in a Jaguar Mk5 and we moved to the upmarket location of 80, Fountainhall Road. The piano was moved to a new front room. Our family had by now matured to the fact that this new front room would be an 'open house'. I did not pursue formal lessons on the instrument but, when my clarinet teacher Bill Spittle visited, he made full use of the keyboard to fill out my clarinet adventures with everything from Mozart to Benny Goodman.

It was only on the formation of my 'Big Eight' band that I finally sat down at the keyboard. Armed with my Reg Owen arranging 'gospel' and checking out the harmonies, I penned out some simple arrangements in the style of Count Basie. I then progressed to filling out some Shorty Rogers and Gerry Mulligan sketch orchestrations.

* * *

The years pass, and in late November 1968 you will find my good lady, Nina and I now moving into a splendid three-bedroom bungalow in Jersey Road, round the corner from the Earl of Jersey, in Osterley Park. Dad had helped me raise the down payment and the following summer saw my parents come down from Aberdeen to inspect their investment. Dad was pleased with what he saw but, with grandchildren arriving and my activities in music expanding, he insisted that the CHALLEN piano should be transported south. Hence it arrived and found a pride-of-place in our living room. In seemingly no time at all, our youngest, Tina, grasped the opportunity and quickly proceeded to pass through all the grade examinations.

At that time, I helped with the early morning school run to the Notting Hill & Ealing High School. In this way we, as a family, became familiar with Ealing itself. We spent every Saturday taking the girls to dancing classes at Babette Palmer's dancing studio, famous for launching the career of her actress and dancing daughter, Bonnie Langford. Annual shows were featured at the Questors Theatre opposite Walpole Park, in Ealing and it was here that Jennifer's school friend Abigail Cruttenden, most recently featured as the TV wife of Hugh Dennis in Lee Mack's 'Not Going Out', also learned her acting trade. Nina and I filled our time, waiting for the classes to come out, by nosing around the local stores. EMI and Bentalls were our favourites, but on the main Uxbridge Road, just across from the entrance to Bond Street, a handsome music store soon took my particular attention. I had discovered 'Squire of Ealing', known to all as simply, 'Squires'; at one time the famed Dusty Springfield had acted as a 'Saturday Girl' in the basement record department.

One morning, as I browsed the shopfloor, I happened upon a magnificent Klingmann grand piano – not quite a full grand, but certainly not a baby. Of German manufacture, in Klingmann's famous Berlin factory, it oozed history and produced a large and vibrant sound. It had to be acquired and in no time at all a deal was struck.

Our CHALLEN would have to go!

The fully serviced Grand was duly delivered and just squeezed into the living area of our bungalow. Tina was over the moon, whilst Nina and I purred quietly as all visitors commented favourably on our unique acquisition.

One special night in Osterley remains in my memory bank. We had by that time extended our bungalow by improving our bathroom facilities, adding an extra bedroom and built-on a quite substantial music room – the new home for the piano!

The Klingmann Grand in pride of place in our GX Music Room

Hello! We were contacted by my long-time musician colleague and friend, trumpet man Dave Holdsworth. We had gone our different ways following the break-up of my Quintet, but we had always kept in touch. Dave is one of those guys who, when nothing seems to be happening, writes his own arrangements, forms a band, hustles his own gigs and goes on tour!

This time they were to perform in Windsor. 'Come and see us,' he cried, adding, 'As we are to be off west on the M4 the next day, to Bath/Bristol and on to Wales, could we spend the night at Jersey Road, Osterley?' 'No problem', we said, and at once set about rearranging the settees and cushions.

The gig was great and Nina and I rushed back to receive the hungry and thirsty band. Nina had pre-prepared a hot late-night stew for supper and, for those with a more delicate appetite, there was always the 'famous' open sandwiches, all washed down from plenty of bottles and cans. The young musicians felt they had landed in a 5 star. On went the jazz records from my collection – heaven!

Our fondest memory of the evening came in the form of Dave's pianist/vocalist – Liane Carroll! She and her bass-player boyfriend were from Hastings, but Dave had discovered them during his days in Brighton. With supper over, the resonating sounds of the piano drifted through from the music room. Liane had found her way to her own heaven. Today she is top of the pile, playing at Ronnie's and all over, winning awards galore for her singing and playing. On that evening, she proceeded to go through her repertoire to our total delight.

One by one the band grabbed a corner for some shuteye. Things were a little slow in the morning, but they all got off safely to the M4 and all-points west.

Fast forward to 1991. With my parents now having passed on and our daughters off to college, Nina and I decided to move out of Town to settle at 'Low Wood' in Woodhill Avenue, Gerrards Cross. Of course, the piano moved too.

It was a quiet time for the instrument. Tina came by from time to time but more and more, the instrument simply became part of the furniture. We invested in the property and our extension naturally included the building of a

Nina (centre) with daughters Jennifer (left), Tina (right), GX, 1991

new music room. Here I gave woodwind lessons, but the piano did not receive much exercise. Then in, 2006, Nina suffered a heart attack followed by a stroke. Fortunately, she made a good recovery, but we decided to cash in our GX 'chips' and downsize to Farnham Common.

But what to do with the piano? I researched the district but there appeared to be no interest in the 'big boy'. Certainly, no music shop would offer us any value, but in typical fashion Dave Holdsworth and his good lady Nell came to our rescue. By this time, they had moved to a substantial barn conversion near Totnes in Devon. Nell confessed that she had always admired the piano and offered to help us out by having it? 'If you can bear the cost of the transport, it's yours,' I declared. So, there we were, saying goodbye to our dear friend.

Now fully restored, the piano sits proudly on a raised section in Dave and Nell's main living room (pictured above). Nell always declares that they are holding it in trust for us. Nina and I have visited from time to time and, of course, to renew our acquaintance I have to fumble the opening notes of Jim Webb's 'McArthur Park'.

***

Afterword

Well. How did all this come about? They say that everyone has a book in them but – where's the 'starter gun' and who fires it?

For me, this was triggered as I was busily engaged in setting up for our 'End of Month' Remix Big Band concert in November 2019. An enthusiastic gentleman of a certain age came up to the stand and thrust a copy of 'Dusk Fire' at me asking me if I was aware of its existence.

So arrived one Trevor Bannister. He had co-authored 'Dusk Fire' with jazz musician Michael Garrick for whom I had played some 50 years past. Trevor was soon to fly to New Zealand to visit his son and family but asked if he could interview me on return.

It came to pass, only a few days before Lockdown #1, that Trevor duly arrived at my home in Farnham Common, armed with his faithful recording gun to commence proceedings and to create the article he wished to compose and publish. However, he had not anticipated that over these many years I had kept a summary record of both, my playing and my business activities. I delved into my Tesco carrier bag filing system to furnish him with print outs and added the promise of more, he would say 'a flood', to follow via email. These uncovered extracts from press articles from my playing days and *inter alia* favourable words about me penned by Steve Voce, veteran contributor to *Jazz Journal* magazine. Coincidentally, at that very moment Steve was compiling a piece on a memorable gig I had once played with the great Tubby Hayes.

Thanks to my fellow musician and good friend John Snow, I was able to give Trevor 'professional quality' recordings of my work on a couple of CDs. John had worked long and hard to extract from reel-to-reel and cassette tape sources some of my better output from live outings and broadcasts. Then only a couple of years back, authored by Malcolm Dome and released by Esoteric records on the Cherry Red label, I was able to pass on the results of 'Atlantic Bridge' now on CD.

It goes without saying that over the years I have shared the 'stand' with many musicians, all of us in our own way, seeking to communicate with each other and even sometimes with members of the general public. What would we do without them? My thanks to all of you for putting up with me and my often wayward and occasional inspirational ways. May I pick out one for special mention?

In my 'truth seeking' days of the 1960s I persuaded brass-man Dave Holdsworth to join me on the search. Even when we went our own ways, we and our good lady wives, have kept in touch. Arguably Dave has been truer to the cause. When I threw my 'toys out of the pram' on the demise of Atlantic Bridge he quietly cajoled me to not abandon all my music. He invited me to join him in some of his jazz adventures. I remember well his project to present his version of the Thelonious Monk 'Town Hall' big band concerts. I still have my charts somewhere. And of course, the chance to share with him a rerun of 'Birth of The Cool' at Jagz in Ascot, will remain in my memory bank for all time.

Over time I have also kept in contact with one or two of my 'old' business colleagues. This took the unlikely form akin to published reports on major sporting events, some dressed up with family background. I was encouraged in this by my good friend Duncan Moore who appeared to find some amusement and solace in the results of my writing even if Wales did occasionally come second.

In addition, on the business front I must acknowledge the help and support of software design guru Ian Richardson and Vim Miller, widow of the late 'PC' designer Keith Miller, for their help with the 'Xionics' story. Last, but not least, my thanks go to Lady Angela Thomas, widow of the late Sir Alan Thomas, who in the midst of all her personal grief, found time to search her photograph libraries to find a picture of Alan from his early 'Data Logic' days.

The result of this saw my new-found literary 'exhorter' and inspiration, Trevor Bannister, leaving Farnham Common somewhat weighed down by all this history. 'It is no longer an article,' he declared. 'It's a book!'

Months have passed in the to-ing and fro-ing of text on the internet and Trevor has helped me to navigate the course leading towards my story appearing in print. He has been ably supported by his wife Anne and assisted by the invaluable help of his good friends, Derek Coller, Tony Hopes and Graham Langley.

Lastly the advent of COVID-19, and the resultant 'lockdowns', has stopped normal life and opened up the time to write. They say it's an 'Ill wind that blows NO GOOD.'

To my reader(s) out there, you can be judge of that!

Jim Philip
January 2021

Appendix:
Jim Philip on Record, CD, Radio & YouTube

Between 1968 and 1971, Jim Philip took part in some of the most innovative and exciting British jazz recordings of the day. They are all currently available, either via online auction sites in their original vinyl format or as more recently issued CDs from specialist record dealers. **Be warned**: the original albums, in mint condition, can command very high prices!

Elizabethan Songbook: The London Jazz Four:
CBS S63512 (LP), Harkit HRKCD 8385 (CD)

'Jim Philip's flute is exactly right.' *Derrick Stewart-Baxter (Jazz Journal)*

Le Dejeuner Sur L'Herbe: The New Jazz Orchestra:
Verve SVLP 9236(LP), Universal 982 014 2 (CD

'And the best is yet to come. Alan Cohen's arrangement of Coltrane's *Naima* with its tenor solo by Jim Philip is the most exquisite thing I've heard since Gil Evan's *Barbara's Song.*' *Steve Voce (Jazz Journal)*

Jazz Praises at St Paul's: Michael Garrick Sextet:
Airborne NBP 002 (LP), Jazz Academy JAZA 11(CD)

'Jim Philip's swirling saxophone solo on 'Rustat's Grave Song' anticipates the popular cathedral work of Jan Garbarek and John Surman in later decades.' *Dennis Harrison (album notes to 'Jazz Praises' CD)*

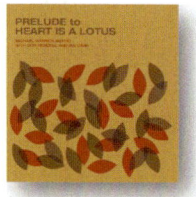

Prelude To Heart Is A Lotus: Michael Garrick Sextet: Gearbox GB 1507 (LP,CD)

'Jim Philip distinguishes himself with his bittersweet flute in the elegiac *Webster's Mood* and eerie accompaniment to Michael Garrick's harpsichord on *Heart Is a Lotus.*' Andrew Cartmel *(London Jazz News)*

The Heart is a Lotus: Michael Garrick Sextet with Norma Winstone: Argo ZDA 135 (LP), Vocalion CDSML 8400 (CD), BGOCD1066 (CD)

'(Jim) Philip is featured on 'Grave Song' over mournful military drumming. He is a fine soloist, with a meaty, melodic approach, and more should be heard from him.' *Richard Williams (Melody Maker)*

Camden '70': The New Jazz Orchestra: Dusk Fire DUSKCD 105 (CD)

'This 'Naima' I suggest is representative of what I call my 'analogue saxophone period', captured here in full.' *Jim Philip*

Atlantic Bridge: Dawn DNLS 3014 (LP), Esoteric ECLEC 2604 (CD)

'Atlantic Bridge is more than an historical curio; Philip and Runswick bring a range of colours and clout to McNaught's arrangements.' *Andy Robson (Jazz Wise)*

Live at Ronnie Scott's Club: The Bobby Lamb-Ray Premru Orchestra: BBC Records REC 116S (LP)

'The duelling tenors of Jim Philip and Tony Roberts wave the flags to close a set which can justly be described as brilliant.' *Max Jones (Melody Maker)*

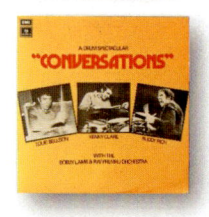

Conversations: The Bobby Lamb-Ray Premru Orchestra: Parlophone PCS 7151 (LP), Vocalion CDLK 4436 (CD)

'I can be heard briefly with tenor man Duncan Lamont on 'Cuchulainn', in the wake of Buddy's near ten-minute tsunami of sound drum solo.' *Jim Philip*

***

Together with his good friend, John Snow, Jim has also compiled two CDs for family and friends, drawn from some of the albums above and tapes from BBC broadcasts:

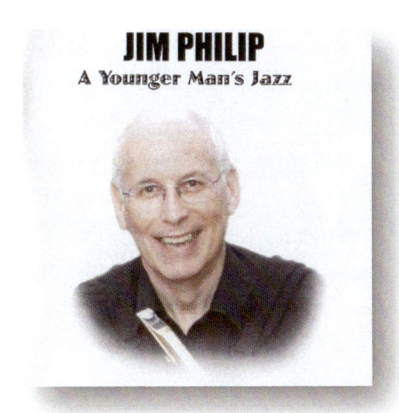

'The Chosen Few' Jazz Orchestra and its later incarnation, the Remix Jazz Orchestra has also issued CDs, again exclusively for family and friends. Jim features on his various wind instruments:

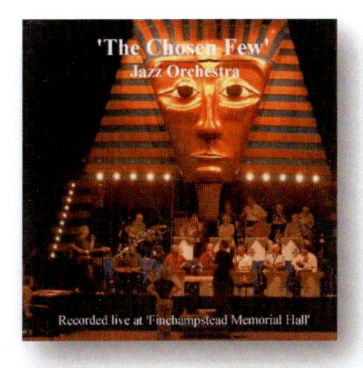

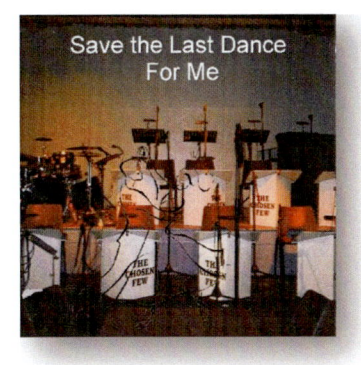

DISCOGRAPHY

The lay-out adopted is the standard discographical one – listing in chronological order, the name of the band or artist heading under which the recording was issued, the personnel, the location and date of recording, the individual titles, the album issue number(s) and the format i.e., LP or CD.

Instrumental Abbreviations

alt	alto saxophone	**arr**	arranger	**bar**	baritone saxophone
bs	string bass	**bs-clt**	bass clarinet	**bs-tbn**	bass trombone
cls	celeste	**clt**	clarinet	**cond**	conductor
d	drums	**dir**	director	**el-bs**	electric bass
fl-hn	flugelhorn	**fr-hn**	French horn	**flt**	flute
g	guitar	**hps**	harpsichord	**keyb**	keyboard
ldr	leader	**p**	piano	**perc**	percussion
rds	reeds	**sop**	soprano saxophone	**tbn**	trombone
ten	tenor saxophone	**tp**	trumpet	**tu**	tuba
vb	vibraphone	**vcl**	vocal		

***

Jim Philip Quintet [2]: Dave Holdsworth (fl-hn); Jim Philip (flt); Mike McNaught (p); Chris Laurence (bs); Mike Travis(d).
   BBC 'Jazz Club', Paris Studios, Lower Regent Street-17th July 1967
Sombrero Sam   *'A Younger Man's Jazz'* (CD)

New Jazz Orchestra [3]: Neil Ardley (ldr); Derek Watkins, Henry Lowther, Harry Beckett, Ian Carr (tp,fl-hn); John Mumford, Mike Gibbs, Derek Wadsworth or Tony Russell (tbn); George Smith (tu); Barbara Thompson (flt,sop,alt); Dave Gelly (ten,clt,bs-clt); Jim Philip (flt,clt,ten); Dick Heckstall-Smith (sop,ten); Frank Ricotti (vb); Jack Bruce (bs); Jon Hiseman (d).
   BBC 'Jazz Club',London-28th June 1968
Dusk Fire   *'A Younger Man's Jazz'* (CD)

The London Jazz Four: Jim Philip (flt); Mike McNaught (p); Brian Moore (bs); Mike Travis (d).
   CBS Studios, New Bond Street, London-15th-16th July 1968
The Old Spagnoletta   CBS S63512 (LP), Harkit HRKCD 8385 (CD)
O Mistris Myne
Flow My Tears
Orientis
It Was Lover and His Lass
Roundelay

Rondeau
Bony Sweet Robin
Green Grows the Holly*
Scarborough Fair/Canticle
The Earle of Salisbury
*Also issued on 'More from the Music of Jim Philip'

The London Jazz Four [4]: Jim Philip (flt); Mike McNaught (p); Daryl Runswick (bs); Mike Travis (d).
   BBC 'Jazz Club', Paris Studios, Lower Regent Street- 5th August 1968
Without Her   'A Younger Man's Jazz' (CD)
Fool on the Hill
Things We Said Today   'More from the Music of Jim Philip' (CD)

The New Jazz Orchestra: Neil Ardley (ldr); Derek Watkins, Henry Lowther, Ian Carr (tp,fl-hn); John Mumford, Mike Gibbs, Derek Wadsworth (tbn); George Smith (tu); Barbara Thompson (flt,sop,alt); Dave Gelly (ten,clt,bs-clt); Jim Philip (flt,clt,ten); Dick Heckstall-Smith (sop,ten); Frank Ricotti (vb); Jack Bruce (bs); Jon Hiseman (d).
       Marble Arch Studios, London-16th & 17th September 1968
Le Dejeuner Sur L'Herbe* Verve SVLP 9236 (LP), Universal 982 014 2 (CD)
Naima*
Angle
Ballad
Dusk Fire
Nardis
Study
Rebirth
*Also issued on 'More from the Music of Jim Philip'
** Also issued on 'A Younger Man's Jazz'

Michael Garrick Sextet: Ian Carr (tp,fl-hn); Jim Philip (clt,flt,ten); Art Themen (clt,flt,sop,ten); Michael Garrick (org); Coleridge Goode (bs); John Marshall (d); Boys from Farnborough Grammar School, University Choir of St Nicholas, Leicester; Ian Imlay (dir); Peter Mound (cond).
        St Paul's Cathedral, London-25th October 1968
Anthem   Airborne NBP 002 (LP), Jazz Academy JAZA 11 (CD)
Sanctus
Kyrie
Behold, A Pale Horse
Salvation March

Rustat's Grave Song
The Lord's Prayer
Agnus Dei
Confiteor
Psalm 73
The Beatitudes*
Carolling*
*Bonus tracks added to Jazz Academy JAZA 11(CD

Michael Garrick Sextet [1]**:** Ian Carr (tp); Don Rendell (sop,ten,flt); Jim Philip (flt,sop,clt,ten); Michael Garrick (p,hps,cls); Coleridge Goode (bs); Trevor Tomkins (d).
BBC Radio 3 'Jazz in Britain' – Maida Vale Studios, London-10th October 1969
Heart Is A Lotus   Gearbox GB 1507 (LP,CD)
Sweet and Sugary Candy
Webster's Mood
Song by The Sea
Temple Dancer
Little Girl

The London Jazz Four [5]**:** Jim Philip (flt); Mike McNaught (p); Daryl Runswick (bs); Mike Travis (d).
       BBC Overseas Broadcast, Aeolian Hall, New Bond Street, London–7th January 1970
MacArthur Park   'A Younger Man's Jazz" (CD)
Same session
Laia Ladaia   'More from the Music of Jim Philip' (CD)
By the Time I Get to Phoenix

Michael Garrick Sextet with Norma Winstone: Ian Carr (tp,fl-hn); Jim Philip (clt,flt,ten); Art Themen (clt,flt,sop,ten); Michael Garrick (p,hps); Coleridge Goode(bs); Trevor Tomkins (d); Norma Winstone (vcl-1).
                                              London-20th January 1970
       Argo ZDA 135 (LP),Vocalion CDSML 8400 (CD), BGOCD1066 (CD)
The Heart Is A Lotus -1
Temple Dancer -1
Beautiful Thing -1
Rustat's Grave Song

Camden '70': The New Jazz Orchestra [2]**:** Neil Ardley (ldr, dir, cond, arr); Mike Davis, Nigel Carter, Harry Beckett, Henry Lowther (tp); Derek

Wadsworth, Mike Gibbs, Robin Gardner (tbn); Dick Hart (tu); Barbara Thompson (flt,sop,alt); Dave Gelly (ten,clt,bs-clt); Jim Philip (flt,clt,ten); Dick Heckstall-Smith (sop,ten); Dave Greenslade (keyb); Frank Jellett (vb); Clem Clemson (g); Tony Reeves (bs-g); Jon Hiseman (d).

'Camden Festival', Jeanette Cochrane Theatre, London-26th May 1970
Stratusfunk   Dusk Fire DUSKCD 105 (CD)
Tanglewood '63
Shades of Blue
Rope Ladder to the Moon
Dusk Fire
Naima*
Nardis
Study
Rebirth
Le Dejeuner Sur L'Herbe
National Anthem and Tango
*Also issued on 'More from the Music of Jim Philip'

Atlantic Bridge: Jim Philip (flt,sop,ten); Mike McNaught (keyb); Daryl Runswick (bs,bs-g); Mike Travis (d).

                             Pye Marble Arch Studios, London–2nd to 4th June 1970
MacArthur Park*   Dawn DNLS 3014 (LP), Esoteric ECLEC 2604 (CD)
Dreams
Rosencrans Boulevard**
Something**
Dear Prudence
Childhood Room

As above: add vocal backing
London-January 1971
I Can't Lie to You
Hilary Dixon**

*Also issued on 'A Younger Man's Jazz'
**Also issued on 'More from the Music of Jim Philip'

Live at Ronnie Scott's Club: The Bobby Lamb-Ray Premru Orchestra
(7): Tony Fisher, Derek Healey, Gus Galbraith, Ronnie Hughes, Kenny Wheeler (tp);Cliff Hardie, Chris Pyne, Dave Horler, Jack Thirlwall, Ray Premru, Bobby Lamb (tbn); John Jenkins (tu); Ronnie Chamberlain, Alan Branscombe (alt); Tony Roberts, Jim Philip (flt,ten); Ken Dryden(flt,bar); Nick Busch, Colin

Humphrey, Tony Lucas, John Pigneguy (fr-hn); Steve Gray (p); Arthur Watts (bs,bs-g); Kenny Clare (d); John Dean (perc).

BBC 'Jazz Club', Ronnie Scott's Club, London-7th March 1971

The Great White Whale BBC Records REC 116S (LP)
Soliloquy
Round and Round and Round Again
Roots
A Winter's Tale
Son of Cuchulainn

Conversations: The Bobby Lamb-Ray Premru Orchestra: Greg Bowen, Derek Watkins, Stan Reynolds, Ronnie Hughes, John McLevy (tp); Cliff Hardie, Keith Christie, John Marshall, Jack Thirlwall, Bobby Lamb, Ray Premru (tbn); Nick Busch, Colin Horton, John Pigneguy, Tony Lucas, Nick Hill (fr-hn); John Jenkins (tu); Ronnie Chamberlain, Alan Branscombe (alt); Duncan Lamont, Jim Philip (ten); Ken Dryden (bar); Steve Gray (p); Arthur Watts (bs); Louie Bellson, Kenny Clare, Buddy Rich (d); Tristan Fry (perc).

Queen Elizabeth Hall, London-5th December 1971

Just Louie Parlophone PCS 7151 (LP), Vocalion CDLK 4436 (CD)
Round and Round and Round Again
Son of Cuchulainn
Conversations with B.L.K

'The Chosen Few' Jazz Orchestra: James Lowe, Alex Brown, Bill Edmunds, Mike Lock (tp); Ross Law, Cliff Luke, Brian Haddock (tbn); Steve Waters (bs-tbn); Brian Marett, Rod Kirton, Jonathan Lewis, Mike Booker, Jim Philip (rds); Jim Pollard (p); Adrian Thoms (g); John Deemer (bs); Bill Castle (d); Steve Pert (vcl-1); Rachel Calandro (vcl-2).

'Live' Finchampstead Memorial Hall – 2006–2007

Jive Samba Privately recorded CD
Lil' Darlin'
Jump -1
That's Life   -1
Straight No Chaser
Hymn to Freedom
So What
Harlem Nocturne
On A Misty Night
Georgia on My Mind
Malaguena

Mad About the Boy -2
Early Autumn
That Old Devil Called Love -2
A String of Pearls
Vine Street Rumba
Dickie's Dream
Just a Closer Walk with Thee

Save the Last Dance for Me: 'The Chosen Few' Jazz Orchestra:
(Collective personnel) Stuart Henderson, James Lowe, Alex Brown, Miles Le Voguer, Keith Spiers (tp); Ross Law, Cliff Luke, Brian Haddock, P. Mattias (tbn); Steve Waters (bs-tbn); Brian Marett, Rod Kirton, Jonathan Lewis, Mike Booker, Jim Philip (rds); Jim Pollard, Steve Walters (p); Adrian Thoms (g); John Deemer (bs); Bill Castle (d); Steve Pert (vcl-1); Christine Jenkins (vcl-2); Francesca McMahon (vcl-3); Lily Deemer (vcl-4)

Basingstoke-unknown date
Privately recorded CD

Minority Ruling
Tuxedo Junction
Don't Rain on My Parade -1
Isfahan
Jackson County Jubilee
I Should Care -2
Perdido
Nicole
Love for Sale
Fever -3
Intermission Riff
Line for Lyons
Charade -1
Willow Weep for Me
Black Nightgown
'Til You Come Back to Me -2
Mr Bojangles
Big Blonde and Beautiful -4
Mood Indigo
Save the Last Dance for Me -1

The Remix Jazz Orchestra: Stuart Henderson (tp, dir); Miles Le Voguer, James Lowe, John Rogers, Alex Brown (tp); Peter Phillips, Cliff Luke, Brian Haddock (tbn); Steve Waters (bs-tbn); Brian Marett (clt,sop,alt); Rod Kirton (alt); Jonathan Lewis (ten); Mike Booker (flt,ten); Jim Philip (bs-clt,bar); Adrian

Sharon (p); Adrian Thoms (g); John Deemer (bs); Dave Lambert (d).

Unknown location and date
Privately recorded CD

Smack Dab in the Middle
Where or When
Brown Baggin' It
Lujon (Slow Hot Wind)
Take the "A" Train
Sweet Georgia Brown
Sidewinder
Some Other Time
All of Me
To Wisdom the Prize
Big Dipper
I Remember Stan
The Days of Wine and Roses
Strike Up the Band
The Jazz Police

* * *

BBC Broadcasts

All of Jim's BBC broadcasts are listed below. They may be cross-referenced with the Discography by the use of a figure in Superscript where they have been issued commercially or as individual tracks on private recordings. The dates indicate the transmission of the programme as listed in the *Radio Times*. In some instances, these will differ from those given in the Discography, which provide the date on which the programme was recorded.

Michael Garrick Sextet: 'The Jazz Scene' 17th July 1966; 'Jazz Club' 3rd January 1968; 'Jazz Club' 24th July 1968; 'Jazz Workshop' 25th April 1969; 'Jazz in Britain' 10th October 1969 [1]

Jimmy Philip Quintet: 'Jazz Club' 8th November 1967 [2]

New Jazz Orchestra: 'Jazz Club' 17th July 1968 [3]; 'Jazz Club' 5th February 1969; Jazz Club 'Live' from the 'Camden Festival', Jeanette Cochrane Theatre, London, 26th May 1970 [6]; 'Jazz Club' 15th February 1971

London Jazz Four: 'Jazz Club' 28th August 1968 [4]; 'Jazz Club' 17th May 1969; 'Jazz Club' 1st November 1969; BBC Overseas Broadcast 7th January 1970 [5]; 'Jazz Workshop' 23rd March 1970; 'Jazz Club' 15th April 1970

Bobby Lamb/Ray Premru Orchestra: 'Jazz Club' 'Live' from Ronnie Scott's Club, 13th September 1971[7]; 'Jazz Club' 'Live' from Gardner Centre Theatre, University of Sussex, 28th February 1972

Further information about these BBC broadcasts can be found by visiting the BBC Genome Project on **https://genome.ch.bbc.co.uk/**

This site contains the BBC listings information printed in the *Radio Times* between 1923 and 2009. You can search the site for BBC programmes, people, dates and *Radio Times* editions.

***

YouTube

Jim Philip is well represented on YouTube as a search using any of the titles listed below will reveal:

- The Jazz Praises Concert at St Paul's Cathedral, Michael Garrick Sextet. This is a remarkable filmed except from the concert, which includes part of 'Carolling' and a complete performance of 'Kyrie'. The entire concert was filmed and subsequently broadcast on French TV.
- 'Rustat's Gravesong', Michael Garrick Sextet
- 'Prelude to Heart is a Lotus' (Complete album) Michael Garrick Sextet
- 'The Heart is a Lotus', Michael Garrick Sextet with Norma Winstone
- 'Le Dejeuner Sur L'Herbe', New Jazz Orchestra
- 'Round and Round and Round Again', Bobby Lamb/Ray Premru Orchestra
- 'Oh Mistress Myne', London Jazz Four
- 'MacArthur Park', Atlantic Bridge
- 'Almost Like Being in Love', The Chosen Few Orchestra with Tricia Bassett

***

List of Illustrations

Every effort has been made to trace copyright holders. The Publisher would be pleased to hear from any copyright holders not acknowledged.

Page No.

- viii. Jim Philip
- xi. 'Young' Jim with my mother and father
- xii. The 'Four Brothers': Bert, Sydney, Alec and Rich with my grandfather
- xii. Rich, fully clad in his flying gear
- xiii. Robert Gordon's College, Aberdeen
- 2. Philip stars for Gordon's in the defeat of Aberdeen Grammar School
- 3. Centre stage as captain of RGS the 2nd XV
- 4. In action on tenor, 1st tenor (2nd from right), with The Jim Moir Band (c.1960–62)
- 7. The amazing Alec Sutherland (2nd left) with vocalist Marisha Addison, Bill Kemp, Johnny Hartley and Laurie Hamilton at a Grampian TV session. Laurie was the guitarist I accompanied to the session in Perth
- 7. Miss Jeannie Lambe, the 'Highland Peggy Lee'
- 8. The 'Munce' Angus Big Band (c.1962). The back row includes Johnny Hartley (bass) and Munce at the piano. 'Big' and 'Young' Ronnie are on trumpets in the middle row, along with Cliff Hardie and Alan Gall on trombones. The front row includes me on 2nd alto and Dave Milne on 1st tenor
- 9. 'The Jim Philip Big Eight': (Above) Neil Simpson on drums. (To the right) Alan Gall (trombone), me (tenor), 'Swanee' Mackenzie (trumpet), Johnny Brechin (guitar) and Johnny Hartley (bass)
- 14. Bobby Breen
- 14. John Marshall
- 14. Dave Holdsworth at the top of the steps to Ronnie Scott's 'Old Place', Gerrard Street c.1967
- 15. *Melody Maker* classified ad for the Little Theatre Club, 11th February 1967

15. Ronnie Scott (left) & Tubby Hayes (right) – 'The Jazz Couriers' c.1959
16. The Mike Westbrook Sextet c.1966 (from left to right): Harry Miller, Malcolm Griffiths, Alan Jackson, Mike Westbrook, John Surman, Mike Osborne. They would 'dress down' for the Old Place
17. The Bob Stuckey Quartet (from left to right) John Marshall, Dudu Pukwana, Phil Lee and Bob at the mighty Hammond organ
19. A *Melody Maker* bill of fare for Ronnie's, May 1967. A small prize will be awarded to anyone who can spot the Jimmy Philip Quintet in the line-up
20. *'Splicing the mainbrace'*, Friday 9th June 1967. Our Wedding Group: John Marshall 'Best Man', Toril Madsen 'Bridesmaid, 'The Happy Couple
21. *Melody Maker* classified ad for the Bull's Head, 4th February 1967
22. My first rehearsal with the New Jazz Orchestra rehearsal, 26th July 1966: (from left to right) Dave Gelly (tenor), Mike Gibbs (trombone), Dick Heckstall-Smith (soprano, tenor sax, flute), George Smith (tuba), me (flute, tenor); Barbara Thompson (flute, alto); Neil Ardley (MD, conductor)
23. The New Jazz Orchestra album cover for 'Le Dejeuner Sur L'Herbe'
24. The New Jazz Orchestra in Concert: (from left to right) Unidentified, Derek Wadsworth, Unidentified, Mike Gibbs (trombones), Neil Ardley (MD, conductor); Dick Heckstall-Smith (tenor), Dave Gelly (clarinet, bass clarinet), me (flute, tenor), Barbara Thompson (flute, alto)
25. The New Jazz Orchestra album cover for 'Camden '70'
27. Barbara and Jon – what a team they made!
29. The album cover for 'Jazz Praises', recorded at St Paul's Cathedral, 25th October 1968
30. The Michael Garrick Sextet, Central Hall, Westminster City Hall, 12th April 1968 (from left to right) 'Shake' Keane (trumpet, flugelhorn), Michael Garrick (organ), me (tenor) (Photograph copyright © Val Wilmer)
31. With the Michael Garrick Sextet. Trumpeter Henry Lowther is in the background
31. Michael Garrick Sextet album cover for 'Prelude to Heart is a Lotus'
32. Michael Garrick album cover for 'Heart is a Lotus'
33. Maynard Ferguson hitting the stratospheric heights
35. Bobby Lamb – trombonist, composer, arranger, teacher and bandleader
36. The Bobby Lamb/Ray Premru Orchestra album cover for the 'Live' recording at Ronnie Scott's'
37. Bobby Lamb/Ray Premru Orchestra poster for the concert with Friedrich Gulda
38. Bobby Lamb/Ray Premru Orchestra album cover for 'Conversations'

List of Illustrations

38. Bobby Lamb conducts the drum spectacular with Louie Bellson, Kenny Clare and Buddy Rich paying tribute to the late Frank King, Queen Elizabeth Hall, 5th December 1971. I am tucked away on far left adjacent to the curtain. A mic stand points to my head (As published in *Jazz Journal*, October 2018)
39. The great Tubby Hayes (post operation) – 'I clung to his note tails'
42. The London Jazz Four c.1967: Back row (left to right) Mike McNaught, Len Clarke; Front Row (left to right) Ron Forbes, Brian Moore
44. The London Jazz Four 'Flute Billboard'
45. London Jazz Four publicity poster
46. The London Jazz Four – an artist's impression
47. Mike McNaught – pianist, composer, arranger and teacher at home in his studio
48. The *Melody Maker* announces the LJ4 support slot opposite Roland Kirk at Ronnie's, January 1970
52. Atlantic Bridge Billboard
55. Me – the 'Day Job version!
55. The Rank Film Processing Laboratories, Denham, West London
57. Young's Brewery
58. Alan (later Sir Alan) Thomas, MD Data Logic
61. Michael J. Bevan
62. The revolutionary XIBUS Multi-Site Computer Architecture
64. The Government Reception for Enterprise (from left to right) Kenneth Baker MP, Keith Miller of Xionics and Tony Davies of CTL
68. 'Nina' at the Monaco Grand Prix, 1975
70. John Pead clinches the sale of the Hawke DL2B
74. The Day I Sold the Car
75. The GP Grid assembled at Barcelona, May 1995 … Get Ready… GO!!
80. The **TOPIX** Consortium Poster
81. Teresa Catlin's support team flanked by Wimbledon 'Queen Bee' Jean Fife (to her right) and my own Jenny Philip (to her left)
84. The beta test AI 'Battle field' display (left) and a Raytheon Defence PATRIOT system missile in test action in the field (right)
90. Delivery Assurance
93. I look on as Gerry Croarkin explains the VISaer project to HRH Prince Michael of Kent
94. The Highland 'White Knees' of Monterey!
98. 'Chirpy' Care performing a 'Chris Ashton' style swallow dive
99. Murrayfield Victors
101. Huw Jones shows his speed, strength and skill to score

103. London Scottish reach for the sky
107. A last gasp. Did Esher reach down for a try?
108. Despondency – Esher win the game but face relegation
110. London Scottish Easter Rugby Camp (above) ... (Right) Luke showing his confident handling of the 'funny' shaped ball
111. An attentive Luke (far right) heeds the referee to calm the 'Heat of Battle', Oxford v Cambridge, Twickenham, December 2009 (Photography copyright © Kickphoto)
114. The Oxford U9 squad, with their 3rd place medals. Luke is 2nd from left in the front row
115. Luke ready for the fray with Oxford U11s
117. Luke with his Cap and Colours
118. Luke in action training with Oxfordshire, summer 2020
119. Phoebe in action in the nets
120. Phoebe stroking a Headington 4, 'Head of the River Race', Evesham, 2013
121. (Left) Solid Defence! Phoebe in action for Woodley Netball Club U16s Team, 2019 (Right) Well done Phoebe! Woodley Netball Club U16s Coach's Player of the Season and Players' Player of the Season, 2020
123. Chalfont Wind Band: I'm standing almost at almost centre stage
124. The BBO Big Band: Syd Busby (left) leads saxes Rod Kirton, Mike Booker (tenors – partially obscured), Terry Bowen, me (altos) and Barry Quick (baritone)
125. The 'Grey Hairs' of the BBO: Mike Booker, Rod Kirton and 'Yours Truly'
125. BBO (from left to right) Jim Hamilton (guitar); Ron Long (keyboard); Adam Linnell (MD, bass); Brian Greene (drums); Simon Campbell, unidentified, Mike Turvey, Bob Hughes (trumpets);Bill Skelton, Toby Gucklehorn, Hilary Spiers, Stuart King (trombones); Prudence Sharp, Mike Booker (tenor); Rod Kirton, me (alto); Simon Sharp (baritone)
127. The America's Cup returns 'home' for the first in 150 years
127. The 'J' Class 'Shamrock V' in action on the Solent in the Jubilee Round the Island Race, August 2001
132. Jack Dawkes, the founder of Dawkes Music
133. Wayne Bergeron, lead trumpet with the Big Phat Band
135. The Chosen Few, Sandown Park: (Back Row) Jim Pollard, Jonathan Lewis, Adrian Thoms, Mike Adlam, John Deemer, me, Dave Shepherd, Bill Castle, Bill Edmunds, Brian Haddock. (Middle Row) Hazell Pollard, Alex Brown. (Front Row) Rod Kirton, Peter Phillips, James Lowe, Brian Marett, Mike Lock, Steve Waters
135. 'The Beast' -the YANAGISAWA B901 baritone saxophone

List of Illustrations

136. Sax Duel at the Surrey Jazz Orchestra: (Back Row) Delia Farrell, Bill Edmunds, Tom Beeching (trumpets); (Front Row) me (baritone), Pete Deane (Current leader, alto), Mike Wilcox (former leader, tenor), Pete Walker (tenor)
136. Poster for Blake's Heaven Big Band, Jagz Club, Ascot, 18th November 2008
137. The Tim Wade Miles Davis 'Birth of the Cool' Nonet, Brighton 16th May 2006: (From Left to right) Charlotte Glasson (alto), Nick McGuigan (bass), Sam Glasson (drums), Tim Wade (trombone), Dave O'Flynn (tuba), me (baritone), Dom Nunns (French horn), Dave Holdsworth (trumpet), Tom Phelan (drums)
138. John Deemer (centre) (Photography copyright © Zoe White Photography)
138. Stuart Henderson (Photography copyright © Zoe White Photography)
139. The Remix Jazz Orchestra, Reading Fringe Festival, 23rd July 2019: (Back Row) Adrian Thoms (guitar); Adrian Sharon (piano); Dave Lambert (drums); John Deemer (bass-guitar); Stuart Henderson, David Cunningham, James Lowe, Chris Preddy (trumpets); (Front Row) Me, Rod Kirton, Brian Marett, Simon Allen, Mike Booker (reeds); Cliff Luke, Peter Phillips, Brian Haddock (trombones); Steve Waters (bass-trombone). Guests vocalist Fleur Stevenson is out of view (Photography copyright © Zoe White Photography)
140. The Remix Jazz Orchestra Onwards and upwards!
141. 'A Younger Man's Jazz' CD album cover
141. 'More from the Music of Jim Philip' CD album cover
142. The Gatefold album cover of Atlantic Bridge
147. The CHALLEN upright
149. Our CHALLEN would have to go!
149. The Klingmann Grand in pride of place in the GX Music Room
150. Nina (centre), with daughters Jennifer (left) and Tina (right) in the GX Music Room, 1991
151. The Klingmann Grand, residing with Dave and Nell Holdsworth in Devon and awaiting its next performance

Index

'**A** Youngers Man's Jazz' 41, 141
Abene, Michael 34
'Aberdeen Angus' 18
Aberdeen:
   Aberdeen Education Department 12
   Aberdeen Evening Express 1
   Aberdeen Grammar School 1
   Aberdeen Joint Station 10
   Aberdeen Press & Journal 29
   Aberdeen Schools Dance Club 4
   Aberdeen Schools Military Band 3
   Aberdeen University 6, 8
   Abergeldie Hall 7
   Beach Ballroom 9
   Her Majesty's Theatre 5, 22
   Marshall Hall 7
   Palace Ballroom 9
   Palais Ballroom 6, 9
   Queens Cross Kirk 29
   Robert Gordon's College 2, 3, 148
Abingdon Preparatory School, Oxon 110, 111
Abingdon Senior School, Oxon 119
Adderley, Cannonball 6
Adkins, Ronald 25
Aer Lingus 92, 93
'African Queen' 5
Allen, Simon 132, 139, 140
Allied Breweries 63
Andersen. Arthur 91
Anderson, Moira 5

Andretti, Mario 7
Angus, Munce 7
Animals. The 24, 49
Ardley, Neil 22–25
Armstrong, Louis 1
Ashbrooke, Roger 81, 95
Ashton, Bill 11, 15
Ashton, Chris 98
Atlantic Bridge 50, 53, 54, 143, 144, 154
Atlantic Bridge (album) 51, 142–145, 153
ATC (Swanwick) 84
ATC (West Drayton) 84
Autosport magazine 67
Average White Band 9

Baker, Kenneth MP 64
Ball, Kenny 6
Ball, Roger 9
Banbury RFC 115–116
Banchory Lodge Hotel, Royal Deeside 6
Barbarians 105
Barber, Chris 5
Barcelona F1 Grand Prix 74
Barker, Mike & Pauline 89
Barnes, Alan 139
Barrow, 'Uncle' Bill 59, 86
Barrow, Howard 51
Basie, Count 6, 11, 148
'Basin Street Blues' 1
BBC:
   BBC Big Band 11

BBC Radio Brighton 47
BBC Radio 2 'Jazz Club' 25, 41
BBC Radio 3 'Jazz in Britain' 31
BBC TV 'Late Night Line Up' 42
BBC TV 'Michael Aspel Show' 42
BBO Big Band 141
Beatles, The 42, 47, 143, 144
Becker, Boris 82
Beckett, Harry 19
Beer, Ronnie 18
Bellson, Louie 38, 134
Bennett, Phil 116
Benny Goodman 1, 6, 12, 73, 148
Bergeron, Wayne 133
Bevan, Michael J. 61–64
BFBS 138
BICC 81
Biffin, John MP 64
Biggar, Dan 100
Big Phat Band 133
Bird-Curtis Quintet 43
Birmingham Town Hall 25
'Birth of the Cool' 137, 154
Black Sabbath 50
Blake's Heaven Big Band 136
Blake, Linda & Nick 136
Blenheim Regatta, Oxon 120
Bobby Lamb/Ray Premru Orchestra 36–40, 134
Bond, Graham 7
Boosey & Hawkes 1
Boston, MAS, USA 79, 83, 93, 94
Bowen, Terry 136
BP Oil 63
Brands Hatch Race Circuit, Kent 73, 74
Breen, Bobby 7, 14
'Brighton Belle', The 10, 11
Brighton College of Technology 9, 11, 12
Brighton Dome 25
Brise, Tony 68–69
British Legion Club, Marlow 124

British Lions Rugby Team 3
Brooke Bond 13
Brotherhood of Breath 18, 19
Brown, Alex 138, 139
Brown, Fraser 98
Brown, Sandy 5
Brubeck, Dave 41, 42
Bruce, Jack 26, 144
Bryon, Kelvin 116
BT 81, 82, 89
Burdon, Eric 24
Burton, Gary 31
Busby, Sid 124, 125
Byard, Jacquie 35
Byard, Jaki 35

Caitlin, Teresa 81
Calcutta Cup 101
Calor Gas 63
Cambridge Lawn Tennis Club 82
Campbell, Glen 43
Candoli, Conte 72
Care, Danny 98, 101
Carnegie Hall, NYC, USA 37
Carney, Harry 11
Carr, Ian 23, 29, 41
Carroll, Liane 150
Carter, Ron 6
Castle, Ben 132
Castle, Bill 134, 135, 138
CCTA 57
Chalfont Wind Band 123
CHALLEN piano 147–149
Charlesworth, Ben 120
Charlesworth, Graham 120
Chalmers, Craig 115
Chandler, Chas 49–50
Cherry Red Records 142, 145, 153
Chosen Few Big Band, The 134, 135, 138
Chicago, Illinois, USA 72
Chinnor RFC 114, 116

CHOTS 80, 82, 95
Clare, Kenny 38, 40, 134
Clarke, Jade 122
Clayton Arms, High Wycombe 124
Cleese, John 63
Clivedon, Taplow 90
Coaker, Carol 67, 69
Coaker, Graham 67
Cohen, Alan 23, 24
Collier, Graham 11, 18
Colosseum 25, 26
Coltrane, John 8, 34, 24
Coopers & Lybrand 81
Cort, Alan 83
Cossor Electronics 59, 81, 82, 84
Cotterrell, Roger 31
County Hotel, Perth 9
Cowes Week Regatta, I.O.W. 126
Cox, Gary 33
Croarkin, Gerry 93
Crescendo magazine 38
Crouch, Peter 127
CSC 84
Cruttenden, Abigail 148

Daily Mail 51
Daly, Derek 71
Dankworth, Sir John 7, 14, 144
Data General 60
Data Logic 58–63, 79–87, 89, 92, 97
Davis, Miles 6, 14, 17, 48, 137, 143
Dawkes, Alan 133
Dawkes, David 133
Dawkes, Jack 131, 133
Dawkes, Jon 135
Dawkes, Lindsay 135
Dawkes Music 124, 131–134
Dawn Records 143
de Beer, Jannie 95
Dee, Simon 33
Deemer, John 138, 139

Dennis, Hugh 148
Dickinson, Phil 63
Didcot Girls' School, Oxon 121
Dome, Malcolm 142, 153
Dorsey, Tommy 12
Downbeat magazine 24
Downer, Jim 56
'Drop the Dead Donkey' 87
Duncan, Malcolm 9
Dyani, Johnny 18

Elgin Jazz Festival 8
'Elizabethan Song Book' 43
Elizabeth II, HRH Queen 125
Ellington, Duke 6, 11
England v Scotland 97–99
Esher RFC 102, 105–108
Esoteric Records 142, 143, 145, 153
Estoril F1 Grand Prix 74
Evans, Bill 43
Evans, Gil 6, 23
Pat, Evans 11
Exeter RFC 111, 113, 114, 128
Exeter University 119

Fairfield Halls, Croydon 25
Fame, Georgie 24, 50
Farbey, Roger 143
Faultless, Ed 43
Ferguson, Maynard 6, 12, 22, 32–35, 72
Feza, Mongezi 18
Fifth Dimension 49
Finchampstead, Berks 11, 134, 138
Fittipaldi, Emerson 75
FKI Engineering 94
Footlights Club, Cambridge 21
Forbes, Ron 42
Ford Formula 1600 67, 69, 79
Ford Formula 2000 70
Forgie, Barry 11
Formula 'E' 77

Formula 5000 73
Formula Ford Festival 74
Fort Sill, OK, USA 83
Fort Worth, TX, USA 83
Franchi, Johnny 22
Franchitti, Dario 76
Fraser, Miss 147
Friden Inc. 56

Garbarek, Jan 30, 58
Garrick, Michael 8, 9, 23, 29, 31, 144, 153
Garside, Ernie 33
Gary, IND, USA 72
Gearbox Records 31
Gelly, Dave 23, 25
Gentle Jazz 126
Geronimo 83
Getz, Stan 49
Gibbs, Mike 18
Gillespie, Dizzy 6
Glasson, Charlotte 137
Golson, Benny 6
Goode, Coleridge 29, 30
Goodman, Benny 1, 6, 12, 73, 148
Goodwood Race Circuit 70, 73
Grahame, Alan 125
Grand Canyon, AZ, USA 72
Grateful Dead 50
Gray, Jonny 102
Gray, Steve 37
Greco, Buddy 72
Greene King Championship League 103
Gregory, Sam 181
Griffiths, Malcolm 18
Gulda, Friedrich 37
Gulf War 1991, The 83
Gunnell, Jonny 50
Gunnell, Rik 50

Halfpenny, Leigh 100
Hamilton, Laurie 9

Hampton, Slide 6
Hancock, Herbie 6
Hastie, Ian 3
Hardie, Cliff 7
Hardie, Gordon 7
Harrison, Dennis 30
Harrison, George 48, 51, 144
Hart, Martin 17
Hawke DL2B 70
Hayes, Tubby 7, 21, 39, 132, 153
Headington School, Oxon 120, 123
Heath, Ted 36
Heckstall-Smith, Dick 23, 25
Hedsor House, Bucks 90
Henderson, Stuart 138
Hendricks, Jon 43, 47
Hendrix, Jimi 50
Hensted, Rustat 30
Herd, Robin 67
Herman, Woody 12, 36
Hewlett-Packard 81, 82
'High Society' 5
Hill, Graham 69
Hillsborough Inquiry 60
Hiseman, Jon 25, 26
Hodges, Johnny 11
Hogg, Stuart 98
Holdsworth, Dave 14, 17, 18, 41, 123, 136, 150, 151
Holdsworth, Nell 19, 151
Hole, Roy 125
Holland, Dave 17, 18, 49
Hollywood Music Festival, Staffs 50
Hoskyns 90–91
Hughes, Nathan 98, 101
Hunt, James 68
Huntsville, AL, USA
Hyland, Al 53

IBM 56, 61, 84, 85
ICI 63

ICL 56, 57, 81, 82, 87, 89, 91, 95
Indianapolis 500 74–75
Ireland v Wales 100

Jack, John 15, 16, 17, 19
Jackson, Alan 18
James, Frank & Jesse 83
Jazz Expo 68 31
Jazz in Reading 140
Jazz Journal magazine 23, 37, 38, 153
Jazz Monthly magazine 31
'Jazz on a Summer's Day' 6
'Jazz Praises' 29–30, 32
Jones, Eddie 98, 102
Jones, Elvin 17
Jones, Huw 98, 102
Jones, Quincy 6
Jones, Salena 31
Jones, Stephen 104
John, Barry 116
Joseph, Sir Keith MP 64
Jubiaba 26
Joustings, Hornchurch 43

Keele University, Staffs 30
Kellas, James Grant 8
Kenton, Stan 11, 12, 30, 36
Kemp, Bill 9
Kennedy President John F. 9
Kershaw, Mike 11
'Kind of Blue' 6, 11
King, Frank 38, 134
King, Pete 16, 21, 48
King, Peter 34
Kingham High School, Oxon 119
Kirk, Roland 23, 48, 53
Klingmann piano 149
Kneller Hall 3
Konitz, Lee 137

Laine, Dame Cleo 53

Lamb, Bobby 34–39, 134
Lambe, Jeannie 7
Lamont, Duncan 36, 37, 38
Lanchester Polytechnic, Coventry 25, 26
Land Rover Cup 116
Langford, Bonnie 148
Las Vegas, NV, USA 72
Lauda, Nikki 69, 72
Laurence, Chris 14, 15, 41, 42, 144
'Le Dejeuner L'Herbe' 23
Lee, Phil 17
Leggio, Carmen 33, 34
Lennon & McCartney 43, 50, 51, 144
Lewis, Jonathan 139, 140
Lewis, Mel 6, 37
Lewington, Bill 124
Le Sage, Bill 21
Lexitron 59
Licensed Victuallers School, Berks 134
Liebman, Dave 17
Lighthouse, Hermosa Beach, CA, USA 72
Linnell, Adam 125
Little Milton Primary School, Oxon 109, 119
Littlewoods 63
Llandow Race Circuit, Glam 71
Lloyd, Charles 14, 17
Lloyd, Harry 81, 95
Lloyd-Webber, Lord Andrew 26
London:
   100 Club, Oxford Street 34
   Arts Theatre, Great Newport Street 47
   Babette Palmer School of Dancing, Ealing 148
   Bull's Head, Barnes 21. 43
   Floridita, Wardour Street 133
   Gatehouse, Highgate 14
   Green Man, Blackheath 22, 30
   Heathrow Airport 12, 13, 17, 71, 83, 85, 93
   Jazz Café 139

Jeanette Cochrane Theatre, Camden 25
Little Theatre Club, St Martin's Lane 15
Market Tavern, Kings Cross 11, 14
Marquee, Wardour Street 24, 133
Metropolitan Police 85
Morley College, Waterloo 12
Notting Hill & Ealing High School 148
Odeon, Hammersmith 31
Ostrich, Colnbrook 34
Palladium, Argyll Street 21
Palm Court, Richmond 43
Phoenix, Cavendish Square 43
Pickwick Club 43
PYE Studios, Marble Arch 51
Queen Elizabeth Hall, Southbank Centre 25, 37, 38, 134
Questors Theatre, Ealing 148
Rank Film Processing Laboratories, Denham 34, 56
Ronnie Scott's Jazz Club, Frith St 16, 17, 21, 48
Ronnie Scott's Jazz Club, Gerrard St 15–21, 30, 30, 41, 43, 48
Rose Bruford College of Speech & Drama, Sidcup 47
Royal College of Music, South Kensington 13
Royal Festival Hall, Southbank Centre 31
Shaw Theatre, Camden 39
Spice of Life, Cambridge Circus 139
St Paul's Cathedral 29, 30, 32
Studio 51, Great Newport Street 50
Torrington, Finchley 30, 43
Twickenham Rugby Stadium 97, 101, 108, 110, 116
Wimbledon Lawn Tennis Club 81
Young's Brewery, Wandsworth 57
London Irish RFC 104, 113
London Irish Rugby Festival 111
London Jazz Four 32, 41, 46–51

London Schools Jazz Orchestra 11, 15
London Scottish FC 97, 102–109, 114
London University 8
London Welsh RFC 97, 104, 114–116
Lowther, Henry 29, 47, 53
Lund, Bodil & Eddie 71
Luyendyk, Arie 75
Lynn, Vera 132
Lyttelton, Humphrey 23, 40

McGregor, Chris 18, 31
McKee, Peter 79, 86
McKellar, Kenneth 5
McLaughlin, John 17
McNaught, Mike 14, 15, 41, 42, 46, 49, 51, 143–145
McRae, 'Ian 'Spivvy' 3
Mack, Lee 148
Mackintosh, Ken 7
Madejski Stadium, Reading 111, 113
Madsen, Toril 20
Maiden, Willie 34
Maidenhead AGRS 112, 113
Mallory Park Race Circuit, Leics 71
Malvern College, Warks 118
Management Dynamics 12, 54–57, 67, 86
Manor Preparatory School, Oxon 119, 120
Manne, Shelley 72
Mansell, Nigel 75
Maslen (née Philip), Jennifer 106, 109–112, 119
Maslen, Luke 105, 109–119
Maslen, Paul 106, 109, 115
Maslen, Phoebe 119–122
Mathis, Johnny 21, 22
Matrix Netball Club, Oxon 121
Marshall, John 14, 15, 17, 20, 20, 41
Maureen Connolly Challenge Cup 82
May, Jonny 101
Melodic Jazz 126
Melody Maker 13, 19, 46, 49

Melody Maker Jazz Scene '68 31
'Memories of You' 1
Micro Logic 62
Midland Bank 63
'Miles Ahead' 6
Miller, Bruce 1
Miller, Glenn 1, 4, 12
Miller, Harry 18, 144
Miller, Keith 63, 64
Miller, Stuart 1
Mobley, Hank 31
Modern Jazz Quartet 41
Moholo, Louis 18
Moir, Jim 4–6
Monaco F1 Grand Prix, Monaco 67, 69, 74, 76, 77
Monk, Thelonious 48, 154
Monza F1 Grand Prix, Italy 74
Moody Blues 47
Moore, Brian (Journalist) 98
Moore, Brian (Musician) 42, 43
Moore, Dudley 7
Moore, Duncan 92, 97, 110, 154
'More from the Music of Jim Philip' 141
Morse, Dave 20
Morrissey, Dick 21
Mosely, Max 67
Mugello Race Circuit, Italy 76
Mullen, Jim 9
Mulligan, Gerry 6, 72, 137, 138, 148
Mundy, John 30
Mungo Jerry 50
Murray, Barry 50, 144
Murray, Connor 100
Murray, Madame 4
Murrayfield Stadium, Edinburgh 99

Nance, Ray 11
National Service 5, 61
National Youth Jazz Orchestra 11, 15
NATS 86

NCR 56, 61
New Jazz Orchestra 18, 22, 26, 33
Nilsson, Harry 43, 47
Norvo, Red 31
Nucleus 41
Nyro, Laura 34

Osborne, Mike 16, 18
Oulton Park Race Circuit, Ches 71
Owens, Nigel 102
Owen, Reg 148
Oxford AGRS 111, 113–116
Oxford Downs Cricket Club 119
Oxfordshire Midi Rugby Tournament 114
Oxford U18 AGCS 118

Paraphernalia 26
Parker, Charlie 21
Parker, Evan 19
Patrick, Johnny 18
PATRIOT missile system 83
Pau F1 Grand Prix, France 74
Pead, John 67, 79
Pepper, Art 6
Perse School, Cambs 11
Philip, Bert 10, 12, 147, 148
Philip, Christina Ann 109, 148, 149, 150
Philip, Jim 24, 26, 31, 31, 34, 46, 48, 49, 51, 59, 87, 92, 126, 141, 143, 144
Jim Philip Big Eight 8, 148
Jim Philip Five 14, 16, 19
Jim Philip Trio 1
Philip, Nina 14, 19, 20, 32, 67, 69, 72, 74, 88, 91, 109, 111, 1 12, 114, 115, 131, 148, 150, 151
Phillips, Tom 82
Phoenix, AZ, USA 72
Piquet, Nelson 74
Plymouth Albion RFC 105, 107
Police Staff College, Hants 60
'Porgy & Bess' 6

Portsmouth FC 127
Portsmouth Guild Hall 25
Powell, Reg 43
Premru, Ray 35, 36, 40, 134
Price, Alan 24
PRO 14 Rugby 104, 105
Profumo Affair 90
Project ASSIST 90–92
Pukwana, Dudu 17, 18
PYE Records 50

RAF School of Music, Middx 132
Raytheon 59, 61, 62, 79, 81–86, 92, 95, 97, 126
Raytheon Europe 59
Reading Fringe Festival 2019 139
Reading University 47, 111
Rees, Alan 67
Rees, Debbie 69
Reeves, Tony 26
Redknapp, Harry 127
Remix Jazz Orchestra 138, 139, 141, 153
Rendell, Don 7, 22,31
Rendell-Carr Quintet 29, 31
Retreat, Reading 139
Rich, Buddy 12, 17, 38, 134
Richardson, Ian 62
Richmond Athletic Ground 97, 102, 105, 109
Ricotti, Frank 42, 47
Rigby, Jeff 47
Robshaw, Chris 102
Robinson, Stan 21, 22
Roedean School, E.Ssx 120
Rogers, Shorty 6, 72, 148
Rolls Royce 63
Rose, Gordon 12
Ross, Gordon 107
Rouse, Doug 16
Rover '75' 17
Rugby World Cup Final 1999 95

Runswick, Daryl 43, 51, 53, 142, 143, 144
Russell, Finn 101, 102
Russo, Bill 12
Rutherford, Paul 18

Sangster, Hazel 147
Schneider, Bernd 76
Scott, Ronnie 16, 21, 31
Scottish Gas 63
Scotland Rugby Team 97, 99,102
SCUD missiles 83, 84
Sebesky, Don 6
Sedaka, Neil 72
Selmer Music Co, Elkhart, IL 73
Semple, Archie 5
Sexton, Jonny 99, 100
Sharp, Karen 132
Sharp, Pru 126
Shaw, Artie 12
Sheepbridge Engineering 5
Shell Mex/BP 13
Shorter, Wayne 24, 49
Siemens 85
Silverstone Race Circuit, Northants 24
Simpson, Norman 1, 32, 34
Simpson, Neil 1, 32
Singer Sewing Machine Co. 56, 57
Singer System 10 Computer 56, 57
Sjoberg, John 2
Skelton, Bill 125
Skidmore, Alan 18
Smith, John M. 60
Smith, Terry 17
Smith's Industries 65
Snetterton Race Circuit, Norfor 71
Snow, John 41, 126, 141, 153
Soft Machine 41
Sole, David 105
Sony Electronics 60, 86
South Yorkshire Police Force 60, 86
Spa F1 Grand Prix, Belgium 74

Spiers, Hilary 125
Spillett, Simon 132, 139
Spittle Bill 3,4, 148
Spontaneous Music Ensemble 15
Squadronaires 132
Squire of Ealing 149
Springfield, Dusty 149
St Helen & St Katharine's School, Oxon 122
St James, Lyn 75
St Michael the Archangel, Aldershot 29
Stadhampton, Oxon 109, 112, 114, 119
Stargrove Enterprises 89, 90
Steadman, David 92, 126
Steel, John 49
Stephen, Ian 6, 7
Stevens, John 15
Stevenson, Fleur 139
Stewart, Andy 5
Stewart, Sir Jackie 69
Stewart-Baxter, Derrick 43
Stigwood, Robert 50
Stuckey, Bob 17
Sunshine, Monty 5
Surman, John 16, 18, 30
Surrey Jazz Orchestra 136, 141
Surtees, John 70
Sussex University, E. Ssx 40
Sutherland, Alex 7

Taylor, Chris 47
Texas Instruments 61
Thatcher, Baroness Margaret 64
'The Individualism of Gil Evans' 6
Themen, Art 29, 132
Thomas, Lady Angela 58
Thomas, Sir Alan 58, 59, 62, 63, 81, 87, 92, 154
Thompson, Barbara 13, 22, 23
Thompson, Patricia 8
Thruxton Race Circuit, Hants 67

Tracey, Stan 31
Traffic 50
Travis Mike 42, 43, 49, 51
Triumph Herald 20
Two Red Shoes Ballroom, Elgin 7

UNIX 79, 80

Village Vanguard, NYC, USA 18
VISaer 93, 95, 97
Visibility Inc. 92–95
Voce, Steve 23, 38, 40

Wade, Tim 136
Walker, Murray 68
Walsh, Alan 46
Warren, John 18
Warwick, Derek 71
Wasps Netball Club, Warks 122
Watson, John 70
Watson, Rod 34
Watts, Ernie 17
Webb, Jim 47, 49, 50, 51, 143, 144
Wein, George 31
Weinberg, Professor Anton 132
Welsh, Alex 5
West, Sandy 7
West Coast Grand Prix, CA, USA 72
Westbrook, Mike 16, 18, 41
Western Park Blades Netball Club, Hants 122
Wheawill & Sudworth 89
Wheeler, Kenny 37, 40
Whittle, Tommy 43
'Whistlin' Rufus' 5
Wilkinson, Jonny 99
Williams, Cootie 11
Williams, Richard 49, 53
Williams, Tony 6
Wilmington, NC, USA 83
Wilson, John 89

Windo, Gary 19
Winstone, Norma 32
Wolf, Toto 77
'Woodchopper's Ball' 4
Woodley Netball Club, Berks 121
Woods, Phil 31
Worcester Warriors AGRS, Worcs 112
Wright, Eugene 42

Xenopoulos, Vasilis 139
XIBUS 62–65
XIONICS 62–65

Yamaha Musical Instruments 124, 132, 133
Yosemite National Park, CA, USA 72